"Bob Fryling is a perfect example of someone whose outstanding leadership is very much grounded in his deep faith. So when he writes about this subject, it comes from both an intellect informed by long experience and a heart shaped by selfless service—a very compelling combination."

Dr. Timothy Johnson, medical editor, ABC News, and author of *Finding God in the Questions*

"If St. Benedict were still alive, he would have written this book. Since he isn't and couldn't, Bob Fryling has. The result is a rule of life formed over the years by one who, faithfully and introspectively, has lived those years in positions of highly visible Christian leadership. Every person in any role of Christian leadership today, however humble or mighty that role may be, will do well to attend carefully and prayerfully to what is written here."

Phyllis Tickle, author of *The Great Emergence*

"Written by a publisher, *The Leadership Ellipse* has insightful suggestions for pastors, politicians, princesses or any other person who has a commitment to Jesus Christ and, at the same time, is called to leadership in any of its forms. Bob Fryling hits the bull's-eye with his reminder and challenge that Christian leaders are ultimately called to have their outer worlds in harmony with their inner worlds—and vice versa! . . . Bob Fryling proves to be a most reliable mentor for leadership in the Christian tradition."

Albert Haase, O.F.M., author of *Coming Home to Your True Self* and *Living the Lord's Prayer*

"Our hearts long for an integrated life. Yet our schedules suggest this is impossible. In *The Leadership Ellipse*, Bob Fryling gives us both hope and a practical handle on how to merge life in the Spirit and life in the fast lane. I can't overemphasize the significance and timeliness of this message."

John D. Beckett, chairman, the Beckett Companies, and author of *Loving Monday* and *Mastering Monday*

"Bob gives us tremendous insights and understanding toward living an integrated, authentic life. *The Leadership Ellipse* is a thoughtful and challenging guide to help us shape our own journey and calling."

Al Lopus, president, Best Christian Workplaces Institute

"I find *The Leadership Ellipse* to be both challenging (dealing with debilitating but often overlooked issues like self-pity and jealousy) and hopeful (chock full of delightful analogies and wise counsel). Read this book to inspire you to leadership which is neither fat with ideas nor thin in practice, but truly elliptical—shaped like Jesus!"

Leighton Ford, author of *The Attentive Life*

"Christian leaders are often devoured by their jobs. . . . The result of this external and internal inattentiveness is often disaster: for organizations, for the people who serve them and for the leaders who attempt to guide them. Bob Fryling has written a wise, honest, insightful book that encourages leaders to take a closer look at their world and themselves. His coaching is invaluable and—by God's grace—will help to bring wholeness and integrity to Christian leaders who too often lead in a fragmented, frenetic fashion."

Chris Hall, chancellor, Eastern University, and author of *Reading Scripture with the Church Fathers*

"Bob Fryling's book is both inspirational and practical. He unpacks the issues and complexities of managing a spiritual leader's life. With biblical and timeless suggestions, it is a must-read for all who want to lead like Jesus for the long haul."

Dr. MaryKate Morse, author of *Making Room for Leadership*

"In *The Leadership Ellipse*, Bob Fryling provides a smart, useful guide for leaders who want to bring their spiritual lives into alignment with their organizational objectives. . . . Over the next decade, leaders who succeed will be people who bring all of their lives—personal, spiritual and organizational—together. *The Leadership Ellipse* shows us how. Every leader ought to read this book."

D. Michael Lindsay, author of *Faith in the Halls of Power*

"With intelligence and wit, Bob Fryling wrestles honestly and graciously with some of the great paradoxes and finer nuances of leadership. This book will be a great blessing to those of us who are seeking to remain faithful to God in the trenches of leadership."

Ruth Haley Barton, president, Transforming Center, and author of *Strengthening the Soul of Your Leadership*

"What makes this book especially valuable among writings on leadership is its richness of detail concerning the fine texture of the leader's life and personality. The weight the leader must bear, in order to carry through with the calling upon his or her life, simply crushes the person who is not, throughout their being, solidly joined with what is good and with God's grace upon all of it. So joined, in ways the author makes clear, there is joy and love, space and creativity, no matter what."

Dallas Willard, author of *The Divine Conspiracy*

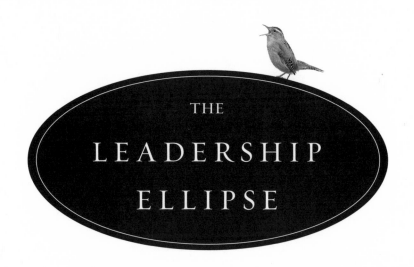

THE
LEADERSHIP
ELLIPSE

SHAPING HOW WE LEAD

BY WHO WE ARE

ROBERT A. FRYLING

FOREWORD BY EUGENE H. PETERSON

IVP Books

An imprint of InterVarsity Press
Downers Grove, Illinois

InterVarsity Press
P.O. Box 1400, Downers Grove, IL 60515-1426
World Wide Web: www.ivpress.com
E-mail: email@ivpress.com

InterVarsity Press® is the book-publishing division of InterVarsity Christian Fellowship/USA®,
a movement of students and faculty active on campus at hundreds of universities, colleges and
schools of nursing in the United States of America, and a member movement of the International
Fellowship of Evangelical Students. For information about local and regional activities, write Public
Relations Dept., InterVarsity Christian Fellowship/USA, 6400 Schroeder Rd., P.O. Box 7895,
Madison, WI 53707-7895, or visit the IVCF website at <www.intervarsity.org>.

All Scripture quotations, unless otherwise indicated, are taken from the New Revised Standard
Version of the Bible, copyright 1989 by Division of Christian Education of the National Council of
the Churches of Christ in the USA. Used by permission. All rights reserved.

"The Peacock" is taken from The Creatures' Choir, trans. Rumer Godden. Copyright ©1976.
Used by permission of Penguin.

"God, All Nature Sings Thy Glory" is taken from Hymns II edited by Paul Beckwith. Words by David
Clowney. Copyright(c) 1976 InterVarsity Christian Fellowship of the USA. Used by permission of
InterVarsity Press, P.O. Box 1400, Downers Grove, IL 60515. www.ivpress.com.

Design: Cindy Kiple
Images: Marsh Wren singing: Stephen Schwartz/iStockphoto
        Peacock: iStockphoto

ISBN 978-0-8308-3538-6

Printed in the United States of America ∞

 InterVarsity Press is committed to protecting the environment and to the responsible
use of natural resources. As a member of Green Press Initiative we use recycled
paper whenever possible. To learn more about the Green Press Initiative, visit
<www.greenpressinitiative.org>.

Library of Congress Cataloging-in-Publication Data

Fryling, Robert.
  The leadership ellipse: shaping how we lead by who we are / Robert
A. Fryling.
      p. cm.
  Includes bibliographical references (p.   ).
  ISBN 978-0-8308-3538-6 (pbk.: alk. paper)
  1. Spiritual life—Christianity. 2. Christian leadership. 3.
Leadership—Religious aspects—Christianity. I. Title.
  BV4501.3.F79 2010
  248.8'92—dc22
                                                        2009042073

P   24 23 22 21 20 19 18 17 16 15 14 13 12 11 10 9 8 7 6 5 4 3 2
Y   30 29 28 27 26 25 24 23 22 21 20 19 18 17 16 15 14 13 12 11 10

To the memory of my loving parents,
Herb and Roberta Fryling,
who taught me to love God and neighbor
and to love doing my work as "unto the Lord"

THE PEACOCK

By Carmen Bernos de Gasztold,
The Creature's Choir,
trans. Rumer Godden

A royal train,
Lord,
more scintillating
than jewelled enamel.

Look,
now I spread it in a wheel.
I must say I derive
some satisfaction
from my good looks.

My feathers
are sown with eyes
admiring themselves.

True,
my discordant cry
shames me a little—
and it is humiliating
to make me remember
my meager heart.

Your world is badly made,
if I may say so:
the nightingale's voice
in me
would be properly attired—
and soothe my soul.

Lord,
let a day come,
a heavenly day,
when my inner and outer selves
will be reconciled
in perfect harmony.

Amen.

CONTENTS

FOREWORD

We have a lot of books written on leadership—how to make things happen in the world. Matching them, book for book, we have books written on how to nurture our souls, how to grow in prayer and attentiveness to God. If we aren't alert, the books cancel one another out, activists taking counsel from those who get things done, contemplatives looking for direction on how to be quiet before God. Christians are well represented in both camps.

Robert Fryling, publisher of InterVarsity Press, has written a different kind of book, a book that keeps both concerns together. Not just side by side but integrated—a serious God-obedient life and a committed society-responsible life. His message is two-pronged: you can't be a Christian activist without being contemplative; you can't be a Christian contemplative without being an activist. With winsome accuracy he has joined two ways of life that are often "put asunder." It strikes me as a remarkable achievement.

Leading people is a demanding responsibility. Following Jesus requires total commitment. When we agree to live what we read in Scripture in our working and praying lives, we soon realize that the leading and following are the right foot and left foot of the Christian life. Omitting either amounts to amputation. We might still manage to walk with a crutch or a prosthetic, but there is no getting around it—we are crippled. When we both lead people and follow Jesus, we quickly discover that the leading and following have a way of getting in the way of each other. We need help.

This is not a book of advice on how to do it; it is more like a personal journal of a Christian leader who has spent his life being a competent leader *and* a thoughtful Christian. This is not easy. Anyone who has lived this Christian way for very long has come across companions who specialize, some in following Jesus, others in leading in Jesus' name. More often than not, they do one or the other very well. Occasionally, we find a man or a woman who is walking beside us who has both a left and a right foot, and we realize that it can, in fact, be done.

But here's the thing: our Scriptures are authoritative that it must be done and also clear about the nature of what must be done in order to live a coherent life of leading and following. This is nonnegotiable. But we also soon realize that there are no detailed instructions in how to do it. Every generation faces a changed culture, different social problems and challenges, new patterns of work, evolving economic and political conditions. Much of what a Christian community in each generation does is learn together how this is done in its particular circumstances. Instructed by our Scriptures, we need Christian companions to avoid seductive temptations, recognize the "wiles of the devil" and assess our particular place in this great, complex kingdom economy of salvation. Proverbs provides no instruction on a proper use of technology. Most of the detailed rules given in Deuteronomy to a nomadic people guided them in navigating a holy life through the Baal- and Asherah-infested hills of Canaan. But those rules aren't much help in the secular world of multinational corporations and working single mothers with preschool children in which we are immersed.

So what do we do? We keep both feet, the foot that leads and the foot that follows, solidly planted in Scripture and Jesus and world, and listen to our brothers and sisters as they write and talk about keeping this left-foot-right-foot life upright. We read what they teach and what they write, books like this one by Bob Fryling (one of the best in my experience) for wisdom and encouragement and companionship in the way of Jesus.

Eugene H. Peterson
Professor Emeritus of Spiritual Theology
Regent College, Vancouver, B.C.

INTRODUCTION

In her book *The Creatures' Choir,* Carmen Bernos de Gasztold wrote a delightful collection of poems putting prayers in the mouths of animals and birds. These prayers express many deep human longings even when associated with the dominant physical attributes of the creatures she chose. She has a poem on the lion and its noble strength, and another one on the swallow and its delight in flight. Though whimsical in style, she is profound in her insights.

My favorite of these poems is "The Peacock," in which this regal bird is debating its own identity. It is proud of its external beauty and presence, but is humbled by its "discordant cry" and "meager heart." The peacock ends its lament with the request "Lord, / let a day come, / a heavenly day, / when my inner and outer selves / will be reconciled in perfect harmony."

The yearning this prayer conveys is consciously or unconsciously at the core of every Christian who seeks to lead others with greater spiritual integrity. But it also highlights the dissonance between our inner and outer worlds. This discord often is experienced in the clash between our outward leadership responsibilities and our inward spiritual lives.

Currently, there is an abundance of excellent books on business leadership, church leadership and organizational leadership that are well authenticated by success stories of size, growth and bottom-line profitability. Many of these books have helped me better understand and practice good leadership principles.

There are also many other valuable books written for how to develop the interior spiritual life. In recent years there has been a wonderful rediscovery of classical spiritual disciplines and the value of feeding and caring for the soul. I have been tremendously helped by many of these books as well. They continue to be a regular part of my reading and contemplative diet.

Unfortunately, much of my experience is that these two worlds—external organizational success principles and internal spiritual disciplines—don't readily intersect or necessarily inform each other. As a leader I have sometimes felt forced or have chosen to live in a dichotomized world that segments my internal spiritual life from my external life of leadership.

Even trying to evaluate these two worlds seems to create irreconcilable differences. Much of my external world is measured by my accomplishments according to planned objectives and goals. In contrast, I tend to evaluate my internal world by a sense of spiritual peace, which is often more a factor of sufficient rest than that of being closer to God.

In fact the very practice of measurement, which is a foundational principle of organizational life, seems suspect in the realm of spirituality. The spiritual virtue of "letting go" seems like leadership suicide. Because of this, I have often felt like the proverbial person whose head was in the oven and feet in the freezer but on the average felt okay!

I necessarily asked myself, *Is the world of success so different from the world of the soul that I simply have to live with this split personality and hope that God is okay with this kind of "average" life?* I alternatively have struggled with the opposite temptation to retreat from organizational leadership because it is too hard, or conversely to reject the interior life because it seems so irrelevant. I needed another way of thinking and living.

A New Mental Image

Throughout my struggles in cultivating a more integrated spiritual life, I became aware that part of my difficulty was that I had the wrong mental and spiritual image of what a life of integrity should look like. I had a neat Western culture's bull's-eye mentality that wanted to reduce everything to a clear point of focus without any ambiguity. My task as leader was to be an organizational sharpshooter that hit the bull's-eye every time.

But that way of thinking and living was limiting and unsatisfying because there are ambiguities and tensions in life that cannot be reduced to a bull's-eye. For instance in orthodox Christian teaching, it is fundamental to believe in both the full divinity and complete humanity of Christ at the same time. It is heresy to believe that Jesus was not fully divine or to believe that he was not fully human. Two seemingly contradictory truths are brought together into the much grander unified truth of Jesus as the incarnate Son of God.

Another example is the classic tension of form and freedom. My experience in organizational life suggests that most of us want structures for others but freedom for ourselves! But without honoring both needs at the same time, organizations can easily become imbalanced or schizophrenic. They become too dependent on structures and control, or conversely too flexible and chaotic. Like the human body with its bone structure and muscles, organizations and leaders need a definite structure to give them strength and stability while also having the capacity to be flexible and create movement.

These kinds of observations helped me realize that I needed a different mental image than the bull's-eye to help me not only understand theology and healthy organizational life but to better understand the seemingly unsolvable conflict between my inner and outer worlds. The mental image that best describes my tension comes from my interest in math: the ellipse.

One of my favorite topics in high school was geometry. I loved doing proofs and solving problems. There is a wonderful clarity and a certain precision in geometry that ironically helps explain ambiguity as well. For instance, an ellipse, which looks like an elongated circle, is defined by two distinctly different focal points that are of equal importance. One point is not inferior to the other, and both are needed if there is to be an ellipse.

THE LEADERSHIP ELLIPSE

Spiritual leadership can be understood as an ellipse. One focal point is our inner spiritual life, our longings, our affections and our allegiance to God. The other focal point is our outer world and organizational life, what we do and how we do it. Together these focal points define an ellipse that circumscribes our true spiritual leadership. It represents the dynamic tension between our soul and our actions, and gives us a mental image for personal, spiritual and professional integrity in who we are and how we lead.

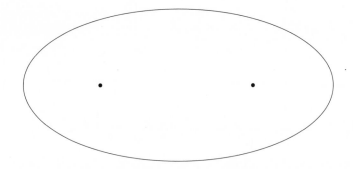

Historically, God's people have emphasized different focal points of their inner and outer lives. For instance, the desert fathers and mothers in the early church practiced their spirituality by retreating to a desert and experiencing extended times of isolation. They wanted to nurture their inner life of the soul away from the temptations of the outer world. Their dedicated example of prayer and solitude is part of our Christian heritage and understanding of spiritual formation.

Many centuries later the Jesuits practiced a far more active involvement in the world of business and education, which was the external focal point of their spiritual calling. Their spirituality can be characterized as "contemplatives in action" and "seeing God in all things." Faithfulness to God was reflected by their advances into the world rather than by their retreat from it.

Jesus' life was characterized by these contrasting practices of piety and activity. He spent time alone in the desert praying, but he also got exhausted in feeding and healing the multitudes. His life was not limited to a singular way of spiritual behavior, yet he always exhibited a consistency or integrity. His teachings and his life were shaped by his relationship to God the Father.

INNER AND OUTER WORLDS

Christian leaders today need to embrace and embody both spiritual focal points of our internal relationship with God and our external relationship with others. We cannot successfully separate or isolate our interior life from our exterior life. Both are part of who we truly are. The more there is harmony and integrity between who we are in the deepest recesses of our being and in the most visible expressions of our lives, the more we will be authentic to both ourselves and others.

But there is even a deeper spiritual dynamic at work in both of our inner and outer lives. It is not sufficient to just be authentic, no matter how attractive that might be at a certain level. Even a criminal or a racist can be authentic if their attitudes of hate manifest themselves in acts of hatred. The flippant criticism to "get real" may be a necessary exhortation to someone who denies what is truly happening, but just blurting whatever we think or feel is not sufficient for personal spiritual maturity or effective Christian leadership.

The Bible eloquently describes and illustrates that we are in the midst of a spiritual battle—the battle between "the flesh and the spirit," the battle between our compulsions to sin and our commitments to God. We have this struggle both internally and externally. We wrestle with what we think and what we say, in what we feel and how we act.

So we may communicate authenticity by being vulnerable in what we say, but we may be using our vulnerability for soliciting the affections of others. Or we may develop our piety in solitude but then control others for our own purposes through our aura of spirituality. The temptation for self-promotion is never far from anyone in leadership.

In other words, our interior lives not only have to align with our external lives but they need to be aligned with the call of God's Spirit in our lives. Authentic spirituality means that we are living with a harmony of our inner and outer lives that together are in harmony with God and his purposes in us and in the world. This book reflects the practical pursuit of living out these convictions.

Part one addresses the focal point of shaping our inner world. One of the main reasons we struggle to live with external integrity is that we are not living with internal integrity. Our mind fights with our heart, and our will may be pulling us in a different way altogether. We then lead with mixed signals on the outside because the signals inside are confused or in conflict. These first four chapters draw from the Great Commandment to love God with all of our heart, soul, mind and strength.

Part two moves to the focal point of engagement with our busy, fractured and surprisingly lonely outside world. The teachings and prayers of Jesus help us to shape our outer world without succumbing to inappropriate allegiances with our powerful external environment.

Part three applies this need for both internal and external integrity to shape us as leaders. It identifies some of the fears that are prompted by our leadership roles but also suggests some practical ways of fulfilling our roles as people called and gifted by God to lead others.

Each chapter identifies a challenge for our leadership and then suggests a practice for meeting that need with a deeper understanding. My hope is that as you read you will be encouraged in your own spiritual journey and leadership calling.

PART ONE

SHAPING OUR
INNER WORLD

ONE

A WEANED SOUL

The Practice of Sabbath

*We could avoid most of our problems if we only
learned how to sit quietly in our room.*

PASCAL

I was not content. I was a vice president of a large parachurch
collegiate ministry (InterVarsity) responsible for the budgets,
training and leadership of 600 staff working with nearly 30,000
students at 650 secular colleges and universities across the country. I wanted to be "on fire for God" but instead I was desperately
struggling to find relief from leadership burnout. I felt physically,
emotionally and spiritually disheveled with all of the competing
external demands of my job, church, community and family. I was
also not in touch with much of anything that was happening
within my heart and soul.

Furthermore, I had no idea of how my internal and external
worlds could be meaningfully connected. I valued both realms of
experience independently, but they seemed in competition with
each other. I was used to accomplishing many things and was
honored for such productive activity. I did not want to lose that

cherished status of "being so busy" by retreating from my world of success in order to focus on my soul. But neither did I want to continue my organizational and lifestyle intensity without a genuine deepening of my inner life.

Consequently, I decided to go to summer school for a few weeks at Regent College in Vancouver, British Columbia. I knew this would be a beautiful venue and thought that just getting away for a while and taking some stimulating courses would be a great spiritual boost for me. In choosing my classes I almost took a course on leadership and another on theology. They both looked interesting and valuable. But I was hesitant to make those selections because my deepest need was not for more information but for genuine inner transformation. So I chose a course in contemplative spirituality called "Quiet Heart, Dancing Heart".

When I entered the classroom for the first time, my heart was pounding. My wife and I and our two teenage daughters had arrived in Vancouver late the previous night after having driven over two thousand long, hot miles from Madison, Wisconsin. I had not slept well, it was raining hard and I couldn't find the building where my class was meeting. Finally, soaked from the rain, I found my classroom and weakly apologized to the class and instructors for being late. I was embarrassed and already feeling like a failure.

But it got worse. During that first day of class, our instructor asked us to draw a picture describing our spiritual longings. I felt both physically and spiritually awkward. Most of my classmates were women gifted in music, drama or the visual arts. They oozed creativity, while the only thing I was oozing was nervous sweat.

I frantically struggled to visually express what was going on inside of me. Not only was I artistically challenged and felt totally inadequate to draw anything either attractive or even recognizable, I was intellectually blank as well. How do you describe, let alone draw, a void?

I was the last person to finish the assignment, but what I finally drew was a scraggly wind-swept tree with almost no leaves on it. Beneath ground level I sketched a complex, dried-out root system. I labeled the picture with the words of Gerard Manley Hopkins, "O thou Lord of life, send my roots rain." That was my longing and plea.

During the following weeks, God graciously began to answer that prayer and sent me on a spiritual journey that is still in progress. We read contemplative writers like Thomas Merton and Henri Nouwen. We reflected on the art of Van Gogh and did liturgical dance. We spent time in solitude and silence as well as in active festivities. We read the Bible and prayed. My spiritual life began to feel more integrated. My mind was stretched, my heart was warmed and my soul felt alive.

Nevertheless, I still had to go back to work. Taking such a stimulating class (pass-fail, no less!) was a great gift to me. However, I wondered what would translate back into the daily life of demands and conflicts I had been able to mostly avoid for a month in lovely Vancouver.

Actually, nothing much happened in terms of immediate tangible changes. The challenges of my job remained the same, the needs of my family were still there, and the pressures of contemporary life only increased in speed and intensity. The world was still tainted with evil, and I was still prone to the consequences of my own sin. Life on the outside was pretty much the same.

What did change, though, was an awareness that the seeds of spiritual life that had been planted in me were beginning to germinate and grow. I was experiencing a life of greater relational harmony with God, with myself and with others. I was growing in the practice of contentment.

CONTENTMENT

"Contented" is usually a wimpy description for a leader. When the

head football coach calls for the quarterback to "take a knee" before halftime rather than trying to score again, the fans raucously
boo. The commentators say that the coach was content with the
score, but the decision feels like weakness rather than strength.

Far beyond football though, we are a culture that likes to "go
for it." We cheer for those who risk new experiences or greater accomplishments. We ignore the past and ridicule the "same old,
same old." We like political candidates who promise change, and
we choose pastors and executives who bring a fresh perspective
and a vision for growth. This pressure for new and better and bigger is especially true for leaders.

Yet, ironically and deep down, we also aspire to be content. We
love the contented feelings we have after eating a fine meal, seeing
a great play or having a meaningful conversation. Sometimes contentment comes quickly after a spontaneous hug from a child or a
kind word from a coworker. We may also longingly muse on vacation, the empty nest, retirement or ultimately heaven as future times
of contentment, when we no longer have to always be on demand.

Unfortunately, such satisfying feelings don't usually last long.
The pressure to succeed is unrelenting and it comes to us through
both external role expectations in a consumer culture and through
our internal human propensity to grasp beyond our reach.

LEADERSHIP ROLE EXPECTATIONS

Americans are the champions and beneficiaries of a democratic
capitalism based on individual liberties and the pursuit of
happiness—which our founding fathers pronounced as our un-
alienable rights. We have thrived on this melding of commercial
success, political freedom and a sense of personal entitlement to
have anything we want. Through our tremendous power and success, much of the world has also adopted such a consumer mentality. We have the World Bank, a global economy and multiple international stock markets.

But such a consumer culture is built on discontent. Companies may genuinely seek complete customer satisfaction, but in order to be successful they first have to create dissatisfaction with what we don't already have. Contentment at the point of purchase doesn't last very long after a new model or style is introduced. Business growth, like fashion trends, thrives on the continual discontent of the consumer.

This pervasive consumer culture places intense demands on us from two different directions. The first is from our own leaders at the top of the organizational chart. No matter what our job, we are expected to always increase results against expanding forms of measurement and evaluation. Our organizations and churches have consciously or unconsciously bought into the Enlightenment's philosophical promise of unlimited human progress along with the practical Japanese concept of *kaizen* or the need for continuous improvement.

This may not be much of a problem on the surface because most of us in leadership are rather competitive. We love the thrill of measurement and successful comparisons. We like to win and beat the competition. We also want to see God's kingdom grow with more conversions, more churches and greater justice in the world. Boards of trustees, elder boards, presidents and everyone in leadership want to grow and be successful.

But statistical success is not always possible. There are recessions, major personnel changes and unfavorable circumstances beyond our control. Also some of us who are good and strong leaders may not be wired to be motivated by external comparisons or the adrenaline of winning. When under too much pressure to be successful, we can easily become jealous, disgruntled or discouraged. Many gifted pastors and organizational leaders have truncated their spiritual growth and organizational success by succumbing to such negative patterns.

Early in my career one leader candidly told me that leading is like riding a bike. Once you get on you have to keep peddling or you will fall off. This fear of falling off is what keeps many of us going, but without much joy or contentment. We may feel stuck, but we just keep peddling faster so we don't fall from our leadership positions.

In a consumer culture we also feel pressure from those we lead. No longer is there an automatic loyalty to a company or church. Just as many institutions have forsaken long-term commitments to their employees, so employees have returned the favor and readily leave a company or ministry if the grass looks somewhat greener elsewhere. People not only use a ballot box, but they vote with their feet and their dollars.

This deeply ingrained freedom of choice that encourages people to purchase exactly what they want, in the size and color they want, affects relationships at work, at school and in the church. People want choice, they want involvement, and they want their own needs met.

This is both understandable and not all bad; participation in decision making and ownership of an institution's values are extremely important. But such an intense negotiable environment can freeze us as leaders. We then forsake true, incisive leadership and succumb to finding out where the proverbial parade is going so we can get out in front!

Feeling squeezed with pressures to succeed from both those we lead and those we follow creates great discontent within us. We feel like the nexus of an hourglass that has to funnel all of the demands from above only to have the hourglass turned over. We then have to perform the same function all over again but now from those we lead and who want us to process their needs and desires.

I assume that we have gotten into our roles of leadership for mostly good reasons. Although our motivations are never completely known or perfect, we probably want to serve others, want to use our leadership gifts and have been encouraged to take on more responsibilities. Leadership is a noble calling, and we have responded to that calling whether from our own sense of vision or from external appointments, or both.

But an unhealthy pressure point for us in our leadership role is created by a classic leader-follower dynamic. In *The Frenzy of Renown*, Leo Braudy illustrates from ancient history through the present time how leaders and followers in all cultures make certain kinds of social contracts that implicitly if not explicitly keep the whole system going. For instance, in Rome people feared the emperor and his coercive power, but they also worshiped him. The emperor gave them security and an object for worship while the people gave him compliance and adulation.

Although we are not emperors we too have our own social contracts with our followers. At first this is straightforward; our leadership role may be well defined by our company, college, ministry or church. We have a job description and performance appraisals precisely so we don't become emperors. We are usually given a honeymoon or grace period to establish our leadership style.

However, at various points along the way, all leaders are faced with the temptation of pretense. We want people to like us and to follow us, although there is this nagging fear that our role is more fragile than we wish and we have to be better or more in control than we truly are. This can be a healthy prompting if we are tempted by a complacency or false sense that we are so secure in our job that we don't have to change or listen to anyone else.

But if our fears lead to overreacting with authority or just pretending to look good, we are like the preening peacock and lose the respect of our followers. We can quickly become a live illustration of the pointy-haired boss in a Dilbert cartoon who is not only incompetent but is embarrassingly self-centered on his leadership image. We may subconsciously believe we are "the world's best boss" because we have a coffee mug that says so!

However, those we lead are nevertheless willing to grant us certain levels of power—to the degree we are committed to them. As the axiom says, "People want to know how much we care before they care how much we know." They applaud our successes but are very watchful of our mistakes and don't forget them easily.

This usually unspoken social contract is real and the pressure can be enormous. We have to be competent and authentic without succumbing to pretense or perks to protect us. I believe this role pressure is one of the foremost reasons many don't want organizational positions of leadership. They are not sure they can stand the pressure of either having to be perfect or living with the critique of not being so. They may want to have the influence of leadership but are not so sure about the responsibilities of leadership—and when we are honest with ourselves, we can agree. The leadership role can bring satisfaction and fulfillment, but it is not an automatic formula for contentment.

HUMAN GRASPING

Much more insidious though are the demands that arise from our own spirit of discontent within ourselves and with our place in the world. Even when we are neither leading nor feeling consumer pressures, we are not easily content. We wish we looked different or felt different or had done something differently. I often wish I knew more or could do more.

This is not a new phenomenon. It was part of the original struggle in the Garden of Eden. There the man and woman, although created in the image of God and in a perfect sinless environmental habitat, were not content with their one limitation of not eating from the tree of the knowledge of good and evil. They wanted something more. They wanted to be wise like God. Later on in Genesis, those who built the tower of Babel did so in order to reach into the heavens and to make a name for themselves. They were all grasping beyond their God-given human limits.

I believe these early accounts of resistance to limitations illustrate why contentment is so desirable, illusive and demeaned, all at the same time. We want to be content but are not content with contentment! As Henri Nouwen once wrote,

> I want to love God but also make a career. I want to be a good Christian but also have my successes as a teacher, preacher or speaker. I want to be a saint but also enjoy the sensations of sinners. I want to be close to Christ but also be popular and liked by people. No wonder that living becomes a tiring enterprise.

Unfortunately, as leaders we can perpetuate and reinforce such unhealthy strivings. We proclaim the good news of the gospel and invite people to come to Jesus so that he will meet their needs. But when they come to Jesus, they find out what their needs are—they need to do this, and they need to do that! In wanting to do better, we seek to know more and to accomplish more. We grasp for the forbidden fruit of living beyond our limits and then impose this grasping on others. All of this grasping, though, only provokes more discontent.

So the roots of our discontent (even when we don't realize it) are within each of us and cannot be simply blamed on others or on life's circumstances, however difficult they may be. But in addition we live with the discontent and strivings of everyone around us, which are magnified when we are in positions of leadership and enlarged even more in a dominant consumer culture. How do we resist all of these internal and external pressure points and find true contentment?

A CONTENTED OR WEANED SOUL

The psalmist, David, gives us a surprising but beautiful picture of spiritual contentment. In Psalm 131 he writes:

> O LORD, my heart is not lifted up,
>   my eyes are not raised too high;

> I do not occupy myself with things
>   too great and too marvelous for me.
> But I have calmed and quieted my soul,
>   like a weaned child with its mother;
> my soul is like the weaned child that is with me.
>
> O Israel, hope in the LORD
>   from this time on and forevermore.

As a father of two daughters, each with two children, I have been around many discussions about weaning—when to start, how long it will take, when it is best for the child and for the mother. The successful weaning of one of our daughters was affecting whether Alice and I could leave her with her grandparents for a weeklong conference we had been planning on attending for a long time. We didn't want to rush her but neither did we want to postpone the inevitable. She made it and we did too.

However, as a man, I didn't have a lot to add to these discussions on weaning. I could listen and ask questions, but there really wasn't much I could do to either hasten the process or add any great wisdom. Apart from some transitional bottle feedings, I was a rather uninvolved observer. Yet even without my direct involvement, the process of weaning happened. It was at times difficult and unpredictable, but it was nevertheless an amazing partnership between mother and child. At some point both had to agree that weaning was the next proper step in their relationship for the proper growth of the child.

David begins this psalm by both recognizing and choosing his own limitations. He is not feeding what Eugene Peterson translates as David's "unruly ambition," nor is he "dreaming the impossible dream." He is not chasing grand, new ventures or drawing up his personal mission statement. He is neither concerned about his success nor his legacy. Instead he has let go of his compulsions for more and is content to be calm and quiet.

This is not the standard picture of visionary, successful leadership. It may work for retreats of silence, but does it work in a board meeting or in strategic planning? Does it leave room for healthy ambition, entrepreneurial vision and stretching goals? Is it just David's lapse into melancholy that belies his extraordinary accomplishments as a leader of Israel, or does it help us better understand why David was a leader after God's own heart?

I confess that I struggle with this image of contentment. I do like to plan ahead and think about what I should do. I want our company to grow, and I want to be personally successful. I like to think of marvelous things. I like motivational speakers who challenge me to think and act more boldly in my leadership. I get a motivational high when I am competing, and especially when I am winning.

However, David's testimony has a clear ring of truth to it. There is profound satisfaction in just resting. Actually, I really only like motivational speakers for their opening jokes. After a while, their high-energy presentations and exhortations feel more like hype than hope. There is a lack of connection with my soul that is hungry for a deeper relationship with God.

Thus I find it both helpful and hopeful that David ends this psalm with a call to Israel to hope in the Lord. By doing so he is affirming that his personal contentment should not be isolated or divorced from the witness and good of his community.

Consequently, our personal contentment should not and cannot be just a privatistic experience. Our souls are to be weaned from our own preoccupations, but not from the people around us. We were created to be in relationship with God and others, and we can't be content for long all by ourselves.

Shakespeare realized this centuries ago when in *The Comedy of Errors* he penned a dialogue between Antipholus of Syracuse and a merchant. The merchant commends Antipholus to "his own content." Antipholus sadly but wisely replies, "He that commends me to mine own content, commends me to the thing I cannot get."

Similarly, the contentment of the weaned child is not something that is attained by activity but is received by letting go while still in the arms of its mother.

So how do we go through this process of weaning? How do we let go of our lunging aspirations and ego, and find spiritual contentment—and especially how do we do so in the midst of our leadership responsibilities? Ultimately, I believe this is a work of the Holy Spirit, who convicts and gently guides us in all of our unique situations. However, there is a well-known biblical practice that helps us to be more spiritually attuned to the grace notes of God's work in our lives.

SABBATH

The fourth of the Ten Commandments says to "remember the sabbath day, and keep it holy." Later on the Lord says to Moses that the sabbath is a sign "given in order that you may know that I, the LORD, sanctify you" (Ex 31:13). Thomas Cahill comments in his book *The Gifts of the Jews*, "No ancient society before Jesus had a day of rest. . . . The Sabbath is surely one of the simplest and sanest recommendations that God has ever made." This reminder in itself is a significant step for experiencing contentment.

When I was a young boy in Pennsylvania, "blue laws" were still on the books, which meant that most stores were not allowed to be open on Sundays. Even Major League Baseball games could not be played past a certain hour, and more important to me I could not play ball myself on Sunday. I did not like this restriction but nevertheless often benefited from a quiet Sunday afternoon of reading. Today, with our current 24/7 shopping and unlimited sports opportunities for the whole family on Sundays, such laws seem both old and odd. Nevertheless, we used to monitor some of what could or could not be done on Sundays.

As my leadership career was developing, I became intrigued and inspired by the example of the Scottish Olympic runner Eric

Liddell, who gave up international glory because of his conviction not to race on Sunday. His story was popularized in the Academy Award-winning movie *Chariots of Fire*.

What was most striking to me though, as I watched this movie about running, was that it was also a movie about rest. Eric Liddell trained hard and was a successful runner. Anyone who has seen the movie can probably still hear that haunting theme music that captured the relentless rhythm of running stride by stride by stride. But the story line was not so much about running as about his courage to follow his convictions of taking a sabbath rest from competitive running.

Although every runner knows that a good training regimen requires times of allowing the muscles to rest and relax, the common image of a champion runner is one who pushes his or her body to the limit and lunges across the finish line. This is probably what Paul had in mind in exhorting believers to "run with perseverance the race that is set before us." Indeed serious Christian discipleship does call for a dedication and zeal that is epitomized by running a race.

But mature discipleship also requires obedience to God's commandments and the disciplines of preparing for our own race with regular times of rest. This is true for everyone but has particular application to leaders who always have more to do than time to do it. We may leave our desks at certain times, but it is extremely hard to leave our responsibilities or the opportunities to get more work squeezed into our days and weeks.

Consequently and sadly, Sunday for much of my leadership life has not been a sabbath for me. Church was full of activities and meetings, and there were always sports to watch on television in the afternoon. I also found myself doing e-mail business and getting a jump on the week with a few extra hours of work on Sunday. I was productive, but not rested, and I did not have a contented soul.

But after my wife and I moved to the Chicago area, we joined a covenant group in our church that was discussing the book *Keeping the Sabbath Wholly* by Marva Dawn. Through this communal reading experience I was strongly convicted that I was disobeying the sabbath commandment with my Sunday activity patterns.

Consequently, I made some changes in my life that are not very strict but nevertheless have been extremely helpful to me. I suspect that I will be learning more about keeping the sabbath, but here is what is helpful to me right now.

Alice and I go to our church for worship and usually an adult education class. This whole time of corporate worship of God and of relationships with our church friends is a valuable part of sabbath. On Sunday evenings we have our covenant group every other week and often will share a light dinner with friends. But in between I essentially take Sunday afternoon off from not only commercial shopping but from bill paying, deskwork, serious studying, e-mail and Web browsing. I take a defined break from electronic and commercial stimulation. I need to have a clean break from my weekday thoughts and activities.

One particularly difficult choice for me was with respect to watching sports on television. Because I like to do so, I used to think that watching a baseball or football game was a relaxing activity, and sometimes it is—unless you are a Cubs fan! But when I was really honest with myself I realized that often after a three-hour involvement with not only the game but all of the replays and the hyped commentary, that I was emotionally tired—whether or not my team won or not. If they won I was excited, and if they lost I was discouraged, but either way I was emotionally depleted. I was entertained but not rested.

I do not want to impose my disciplines on others, as we all need to sort out for ourselves what is restful and what is not. But even as a sports fan, I do think that there is a level of idolatry and time consumption with sports that robs our souls of energy and spiritual vitality. Of course there are other idolatries for nonsports fans, like excessive shopping or movie going, which seem relaxing at first but can also weary our bodies and souls. The issue is not to be legalistic for each other but to be attentive to what is truly restful and provides the environment for a quiet heart.

Journaling can help provide such an environment. Although I am not someone who journals avidly, it has become something that is both quieting and helpful to me. I usually do my journaling on my sabbath. I write in my journal what I am thinking and feeling about my spiritual life. Sometimes I reflect on that day's sermon or what I have been reading in Scripture. Sometimes I simply identify struggles or desires. I then take time to reflectively pray while sitting in a comfortable chair or when taking a walk. I find it helpful to pray out loud. I also feel free to read or take a nap.

In an article by Philip Yancey, I came across a story about Yo-Yo Ma, the world-class cellist. Evidently, Yo-Yo plays a Bach suite from memory every night before going to bed. He says, "This isn't practicing, it's contemplating. You're alone with your soul." For me, my journal is like his cello, and journaling is a regular opportunity to be alone with my soul.

A side benefit of having sabbath rest is that we are better equipped to handle difficult and intrusive events in our lives. One of the members of our covenant group that was reading and discussing Marva Dawn's book was a theology professor. He openly acknowledged that he often used Sundays to do lesson plans for the following week but felt convicted that he shouldn't do this. So he changed his work patterns so that he could have a sabbath away from his teaching responsibilities.

At the end of the academic year, my wife asked him what difference this lifestyle change had made for him. He replied that not only did he feel more rested, he didn't get hooked on departmental politics as much! The secondary benefit for him in addition to physical rest was a rest to his ego and soul.

Many years ago Eugene Peterson wrote a provocative article in

Leadership called "The Unbusy Pastor." In it he said, "The word busy is the symptom not of commitment but of betrayal." He then quoted John Oman, who said, "The twin perils of ministry are flurry and worry. Flurry dissipates energy while hurry constipates it!"

Along a similar vein John Ortberg, pastor of Menlo Park Presbyterian Church, tells the story of asking USC professor of philosophy Dallas Willard what is needed to be spiritually healthy. Dallas replied, "You must ruthlessly eliminate hurry from your life." That may sound like the privilege of a tenured professor, but there is a reason why people not only want to listen to Dallas but to be with him as well. He is not any less busy, but his unhurried presence reflects his spiritual depth.

 The sabbath is not a suggestion but a command to cease our work. It bears the same weight of biblical authority as the other Ten Commandments, such as "do not kill" or "do not commit adultery." We rationalize our avoidance of obeying this command at our own spiritual, emotional and physical risk.

Yet it is not to be taken legalistically. In one of Jesus' teachings on sabbath he supported his disciples for picking grain to eat on the sabbath in the face of accusations from the law-watching Pharisees. He quotes from Hosea in the Old Testament that what God most desires is "mercy and not sacrifice." He concludes that the sabbath was made for us and not us for the sabbath.

But I believe we need to help each other with this in not only being accountable to each other but also just in reducing the amount of work we give each other. More specifically, if the axiom "work expands to the amount of time allotted to it" is true, then resting one day in seven actually eliminates one-seventh or 14 percent of our work! Like an athlete who plays within his or her limits, living according to our God-created limits multiplies our effectiveness. A friend of mine told me to remember that fallowness comes before fruitfulness, both in the dictionary and in the spiritual life.

However, taking a sabbath is not a leadership principle that is one more thing "to do" or even a strategy for being more successful. If we use the sabbath as a means to the end of greater productivity, we have lost the spirit of sabbath, which is to cease from our work that we may find "rest for our souls" as well as physical rest. One of the greatest temptations and problems we experience in leadership is competing with other leaders, with other pastors and with those in our organizations. We long to be recognized and work harder, or we try to control situations so that we stand out above others.

But the harder we work, the less we feel loved because we don't have the time to receive love from others and especially from God. Our lives are so full at an external level that we don't have the capacity to absorb what is far more satisfying to our hearts and souls. The great African theologian Augustine observed that we don't open our arms to receive from God because they are already so full with our own concerns.

We also may not have time to listen well to others or to respond to their needs. Sometimes we work so hard and sacrifice our emotional attentiveness to others that we cannot extend mercy to them. We are far more uptight and feisty when we are overworking than when we are rested.

Putting this all together, I have tried to live what I call a "sabbath lifestyle" that not only takes a weekly sabbath but also tries to monitor and adjust the quietness of my heart. When I get too combative with others or discouraged with myself, it is almost always an indication that my soul is not quiet or content.

Sabbath keeping is not a panacea for all of our anxieties and discontents, but it is that tangible, weekly reminder that God is God and we are not. There is an old Jewish saying that "the sabbath has kept the Jews more than the Jews have kept the sabbath." Maybe that is true for us as well. Sabbath keeping is countercultural in our 24/7 world. But it is a practice that weans us from our infantile need for immediate gratification and allows for a deeper contentment of our souls.

TWO

A Growing Strength

The Practice of Pruning

With the help of the thorn in my foot,
I spring higher than anyone with sound feet.

SØREN KIERKEGAARD

Our leadership ellipse diagrams the intersection of what is happening in our souls and what is happening in our leadership. However, it can also illustrate a creative tension around growth and at times the need to refrain or cut back from growing.

Growth is a leadership assumption and aspiration. We want our churches to grow; we want our companies, our institutions and our ministries to grow. We want to grow our bottom line, our market share, our brand name and our reputation. Growth is good and necessary for economic and organizational health. Growth is a fundamental part of our leadership responsibilities.

Similarly, we want to grow as an individual in our intellectual, physical and spiritual capacities. Our presumed personal growth curve is always going up despite some of the harsh realities of midlife limits and fears of our "declining years." Even when we accept that our bodies are on a downward slope as life goes on, we have this hope of continual spiritual growth culminating in an eternity of soul satisfaction.

But this does not happen automatically. The testimony of those who work with the elderly is that the spiritual life does not necessarily become stronger with age. However, it becomes more visible because we lose our ability to hide what is going on inside of us. We become more like children in our transparency to others. If we have been self-centered and insensitive to others in our past, we will become even more noticeably so as life goes on.

Conversely, if we have been loving and caring for others in our lives, we will likely continue to exhibit those virtues when we may not even know we are doing so. My mother was such a person even though aging was a difficult experience for her. She hated to let go of things and often would comment that she felt fine except for her body!

But even in times of discouragement in her nursing home, she would reach out to the nurses' aides to find out about their families and then quietly pray for them. Shortly before Mom died, the chaplain told me that she would often stop by to see mom because Mom was such an encouragement to her. Rather than demanding the chaplain's time, Mom was interested in her and all of the people she had to visit. She didn't want to take the chaplain away from her job.

It seems that the seeds we sow throughout our lives not only sprout when we can see them, but they continue to blossom when we are not looking or when our eyesight is dim. When I was a boy, Mom used to repeat the words of the apostle Paul, "Do not be deceived; God is not mocked, for you reap whatever you sow" (Gal 6:7). I am profoundly grateful that both my mom and dad sowed seeds of righteousness in their lives and mine.

LEGACY AND REPUTATION

However, my struggle now is not so much what I will be like in a nursing home, although I do want to be like Mom and Dad and others who exhibit God's grace most clearly when they are least able to fake it. I want my life and my legacy to be strong. I care for who I am becoming and the good I will leave behind.

My struggle is with some of the reasons for those desires. Under the veneer of leaving a vibrant spiritual legacy, these desires can still be ego-centered and prideful ways of trying to control what other people think of me. Such desires can quickly lead to distorted behaviors of pretense, posturing and denial. They look beautiful in principle but readily wilt under the glare of daily organizational decisions and relationships. Do I make decisions for what is best for others or what is best for my reputation?

This ethical conflict is often glaring in politicians. I recently read a biography of Andrew Jackson, who rose from a poor background to become a powerful American president. At the end of his second term, Jackson was driven to unify the country. But in doing so, he ignored the plight of the slaves and set in motion the horrendous "trail of tears" that forced the relocation and death of thousands of Cherokee Indians. His popular reputation at the time has been greatly diminished in the eyes of history, because of his moral compromises.

But he and other politicians are not the only leaders that become fixated and trapped by a preoccupation with either legacy or just what other people think about them on a daily basis. This is endemic to leadership positions because we are so dependent for our success on how our followers think and talk about us. We consequently feel tremendous pressures to either placate or capitulate to our followers so that they will not only like us but will not turn against us.

What makes this pressure so complicated is that our motivation in responding to it is never pure. We know that selfish motivation will never take us far in Christian leadership and most of us don't want to be self-centered. We try to guard against it. We may also truly want to promote our followers and go to bat for them as a good leadership practice and with a genuine concern for them. Caring for and listening to our followers and honoring them are essential traits of good leaders. An insidious threat to our spiritual health, though, comes not so much from a lack of good desires but from a lack of self-awareness of being driven and controlled by underlying selfish interests. Good leaders are usually very aware of what is happening inside of them.

Abraham Lincoln was such a leader. He was known for his ability to understand and empathize with not only his friends but also his detractors and enemies. Doris Kearns Goodwin wrote a 916-page *New York Times* Best Seller, *Team of Rivals*, that was based on Lincoln's tremendous ability to bring together diverse and egocentric leaders—including those who ran directly against him for his presidential nomination. She emphasized this rare leadership gift through the book's subtitle: *The Political Genius of Abraham Lincoln*.

But Lincoln was not only aware of the flaws and motivations of others. He also knew himself. Doris Kearns Goodwin writes about a time when Lincoln stopped and walked back half a mile to rescue a pig caught in a mire. He did not do this because he loved the pig, recollected a friend, but "just to take a pain out of his own mind." Lincoln didn't pretend he was being totally altruistic in rescuing this pig. His conscience got the best of him, and he wanted to be able to sleep that evening.

I am becoming increasingly aware of the importance of listening to those blips of conscience throughout the day. Recently I heard that a senior publishing executive had lost her job. I did not know her as a close friend, but because she is an Orthodox Jew and observed Shabbat faithfully, we have had several good conversations about the sabbath. She also reminds me of the mothers of my boyhood Jewish friends. With her forced retirement, I probably will never see her again and didn't need to do a thing about her termination. But I did feel a certain kinship with her and was prompted to track her down just to say I was sorry to hear of her job loss and how I would miss seeing her at publishing events. This was not an efficient use of my time with respect to my job, but it was tremendously satisfying to make a much deeper human connection with her.

There are also the times when I need to apologize, or not write that defensive e-mail. If I am moving too fast I may not even hear the blips or take time to respond to them. Or I may think too highly of myself for doing so, which leads to a false pride and distorted relationships. Honest self-awareness prompted by the Holy Spirit is one of the greatest leadership resources we have.

LEADERSHIP PASSIONS

In his popular book *True North*, Bill George states that we need to lead according to our passions if we are to be authentic and effective in our leadership. He says, "no one can be authentic by trying to be like someone else," and "successful leadership takes conscious development and requires being true to your life story." In a similar vein I like the quip of Oscar Wilde, "Be yourself. Everybody else is taken."

There is much wisdom in this perspective. God has given us gifts and abilities, and we should boldly use these attributes in our leadership. There is great freedom and success in living out of our strengths. In fact when we don't, we feel stifled and unproductive. We are like left-handed people trying to write with our right hands.

But what is missing in this analysis is our unhealthy passions. What if what we want to do sometimes is not particularly meaningful or maybe even wrong? Can we always trust our passions?

A rather neutral example of the limits of this kind of "go with your passion" kind of thinking happened when I dutifully tried to follow an exercise in George's book about identifying the times in my life when I was most alive and happy. The first thing that came to my mind was when I got my first and only hole-in-one in golf.

I was playing with a friend from church and on the seventeenth hole of a local course. I hit a 4 iron 163 yards right into the hole. It was a great thrill to get a hole in one, and I do have some passion for playing golf. I thoroughly enjoy the exercise and the unrelenting challenge of the game. But I could never build my life around golf. It is very temporary and limited in its ability to give lasting satisfaction. It is not my true north. It is not what I am primarily called to do.

More significantly, we can also clearly have negative passions and addictions, such as alcohol abuse, marital infidelities and financial greed that so often derail leaders. If their wrenching testimonies are valid, these leaders did not intend to abuse their power or ruin their marriages, but they became immune to knowing what was right and wrong and followed their lustful passions without restraint.

Other passions that are not so socially reprehensible but can be just as relationally destructive are envy or jealousy or controlling other people by dominating conversations with them. There is a reason why Scripture and classic spirituality often link our passions with our sinful rather than our sanctified natures.

DIVINE DISCERNMENT

So how do we enthusiastically follow our God-given passions without being undercut by our passions that are tainted by sin? The bookend verses of Psalm 139 have been of great value to me in seeking such spiritual discernment. The last verses are the most familiar, with David praying:

> Search me, O God, and know my heart;
>   test me and know my thoughts.
> See if there is any wicked way in me,
>   and lead me in the way everlasting. (vv. 23-24)

These words express the honest longings of David to discern

who he is in his innermost being. It is one of the most significant prayers we can utter.

But the preceding verses of that psalm give a context that makes the last few verses even more important. The psalm begins with

> O LORD, you have searched me and known me.
> You know when I sit down and when I rise up;
>   you discern my thoughts from far away. (vv. 1-2)

The rest of the psalm adds further evidence of God's omniscience that in one way makes the concluding prayer unnecessary. The Lord doesn't need our invitation to know us. He already knows our intricacies beyond our own comprehension. The prayer then at the end is recognition of God's knowledge and a desire on the part of David to be part of that awareness. David's conclusion—"lead me in the way everlasting"—recognizes that all of our desires and passions are not completely pure, and that we need God's direction to guide our choices.

In my best moments I want this. But as the apostle Paul testifies to the Christians at Rome, there are times when this just doesn't happen. He says, "I do not do the good I want, but the evil I do not want is what I do" (Rom 7:19). How do we escape this bondage of conflicting desires?

Ultimately, as Paul goes on to say, it is the Holy Spirit who releases us from such bondage. But we know this is not a one-time magical solution imposed on us. The witness of the Scriptures, and the saints like John Bunyan in his classic *Pilgrim's Progress*, is that the spiritual life is a journey with many detours and difficulties. Our spiritual strength is not dependent on our success and willfulness to do what is right but on our willingness to receive God's righteousness in the midst of all the hardships we experience along the way.

In fact many of the metaphors of Scripture for the spiritual life are not of ever-increasing passionate growth free from pain or limitations. Rather they are pictures of sacrifice, of cutting back and letting go. For instance, there is the Old Testament story of how the Israelite leader Gideon routed the Midianites by reducing his forces from thirty thousand soldiers to three hundred so they would credit the Lord for their victory. It is counterintuitive in our culture of acquisition, but less can indeed be more. A disciplined if painful cutting away of something that seems to be very important to us is often the necessary path of godly maturity.

CIRCUMCISION AS A SPIRITUAL METAPHOR

Another even more dramatic picture in Scripture for spiritual fidelity is that of circumcision. It was first instituted by God as a literal sign of God's unique relationship with Abraham and his descendants. It was not like puberty rites in other cultures that just celebrated the individual's coming of age within a community. Rather it was a sign of God's covenant to his people and their allegiance to him.

A little further on in Israel's history, circumcision became a spiritual metaphor for faithfulness. At the end of Moses' life, as he is giving his final teachings to the children of Israel, Moses proclaims that "the LORD your God will circumcise your heart . . . so that you will love the LORD your God with all your heart and with all your soul, in order that you may live" (Deut 30:6).

When Moses said this, he wasn't just speaking to men, despite the male metaphor. Nor was he giving a retirement speech of platitudes. He was revealing something of God's intentions for all those who seek to follow God. This was so much so that uncircumcision was a metaphor for impurity and unfaithfulness. Moses spoke of his "uncircumcised lips" (Ex 6:12) that were unable to speak well for God, and Jeremiah talks about uncircumcised ears that inhibited hearing God (Jer 6:10).

The apostle Paul picks up on this in his letter to the Romans and argues that true circumcision or even being Jewish is not primarily a matter of outward, physical circumcision. He concludes that "a person is a Jew who is one inwardly, and real circumcision is a matter of the heart—it is spiritual and not literal" (Rom 2:29).

Despite its frequency in Scripture, though, circumcision is a metaphor that is embarrassing to talk about—and especially in mixed company. It is so private and sexual in nature. But maybe that is part of the reason it is used so often in Scripture and is so relevant. We don't mind talking about our more presentable spiritual attributes of commitment and zeal, but we don't like to talk about what is very private and painful to our identity, like our fears and our doubts. These may be hidden in our private journals, but the aura of leadership we covet demands a more positive spin—not just because that is our desire but it is what our followers seem to want in us as well.

When former president Jimmy Carter admitted to feeling a certain malaise in the country, he was ridiculed and at that point lost an edge to his leadership credibility. This is scary to us as leaders. We don't want to appear weak or not upbeat. We want to inspire vision and "go for the gold." We want to be and appear to be confident and competent.

But true Christian leadership requires a certain level of vulnerability in our spiritual lives. In the Psalms David laments his sins in leadership. The apostle Paul candidly wrote about his physical and spiritual struggles, and Augustine wrote a whole book about his life that he appropriately called his *Confessions*.

I readily admit that I don't know how to fully express such spiritual authenticity in my leadership. I want to be genuine but I am also aware of the temptation to be vulnerable so that the vulnerability itself becomes manipulative in how I want people to see me. This reality may not be so true in the marketplace but is often true in the church or other Christian settings. The temptation in either setting, though, is to be more concerned for what our followers think than about being genuine in our relationship with God and others. For this we need spiritual circumcision.

PRUNING AS A SPIRITUAL METAPHOR

Another and more acceptable biblical metaphor for spiritual growth is that of pruning. While circumcision relates to our deeply private relationship with God, pruning is more public. In Jesus' famous teaching about the vine grower, the true vine and the vine branches, he unapologetically talks to his disciples about pruning branches so they will bear fruit.

Jesus' desire for his followers is not one of leafy growth with little or no fruit. Like his first command to the man and woman in the Garden of Eden, "Be fruitful and multiply," God also wants us to be fruitful in our lives. But fruitfulness requires pruning, whether the pruning of the desire to eat of that original forbidden tree or the pruning of our contemporary desires to be like God.

Several years after Alice and I were married, we were invited to a marriage seminar led by Walter and Ingrid Trobisch. They were part of an international Lutheran mission and did extensive marriage counseling in North America, Europe and Africa. This broad experience gave them rich insights and practical wisdom in their teaching and counseling.

Once as Walter was talking about the normal difficulties to be expected in marriage, he shared his deep conviction that "without pain, there is no growth." This was hard to hear because no one wants pain in marriage. But Alice and I have come to greatly value this insight—it gives us hope and perseverance to work through the pain of our problems rather than avoid or deny them. Like a woman in labor who finds that the expectation of having her baby in her arms helps sustain her through the pain of childbirth, so we who hope to have abundant life in Christ must too accept the pain of God's creative work within us.

This desire for a genuine spiritual growth has led me to recognize three temptations that need to be pruned away for me to find freedom in my spirit and my leadership. Although we each face our own temptations and unique struggles, I have observed that these three issues seem characteristic of almost all leaders because they are rooted in pride, which Augustine called "the mother of all heretics."

Pruning of reputation and self-righteousness. I need to be pruned from having to be right, which easily becomes self-righteousness. This is a prevailing sin among all leaders and especially among the religious. Part of our job is to discern what is right or wrong and live life accordingly. This is not what causes sin. It is rather the self-satisfied conclusions and pronouncements that we have reached a stage of perfection that opens the door for self-righteousness to enter into our attitudes and behaviors.

This is what Jesus condemned among the Pharisees when he called them "whitewashed tombs." Their concern for their reputation and exemplary piety was covering over their inner selfishness. They were like the peacock who had beautiful plumage on the outside but had an ugly, raucous cry inside. It is no surprise that the hypocrisy, or even the perceived hypocrisy, of dedicated believers continues to be a major reason for others rejecting religious faith.

In talking about the need to be right and responsible in my job accountabilities, I'm not suggesting that the option of being wrong and irresponsible is the way to go! Rather I am referring to my self-perceptions that I invariably and often unconsciously communicate to others. I have reluctantly and painfully discovered that when I have allowed my job role and leadership responsibilities to define my sense of self, I have lost perspective and to some degree my leadership effectiveness.

Perhaps because I have spent much of my life connected with the university world, I value the laudable academic mindset of pursuing truth. I enjoy the stimulation of vigorous debate and wrestling with ideas. Unfortunately an unbridled pursuit of truth without a humble understanding of self often becomes a clash of egos to prove who is right or better. Sadly I have all too frequently imbibed that spirit of wanting to win every argument for "the sake of truth" and using it as a weapon on others or a platform for self-promotion.

Yet I can't fully blame the academy for this combative inclination. When I graduated from high school I was unnerved when I read the personal yearbook comments of a girl I had known for many years. We had never dated but we did things like orchestra and calculus together, and I had often talked with her about becoming a Christian. Like most high school seniors we traded yearbooks with our friends to collect signatures and good wishes. I was stunned when I read her comment to me "Love to a great guy, but oh so argumentative"!

Her comment obviously has stuck with me. It is a reminder of how my weaknesses are so deeply entrenched. Part of what was healing for me in this situation is that many years later I tracked this friend down to apologize to her for my argumentative behavior. She was a doctor with two kids. She seemed both surprised and deeply touched by my confession, and I still hope that one day she will be able to fully receive God's love for her.

But the same spirit of winning or being right also dominates business strategy and practice. Sports metaphors and sports heroes have become normal reference points for both Christian and secular leadership contexts. Climbing the ladder in the corporate world often includes the necessity of pushing others off the ladder. Competition can be fierce and not always friendly. Ego battles in the legal and medical professions is legendary and the brunt of many jokes.

Sadly this is also true in the church world as well. Pastors compete with other pastors. Theologians fight other theologians. When the great church Reformer John Calvin was in school, his

Latin buddies referred to him as "The Accusative Case" because of the way he always seem to challenge what they said. Even today many devoted followers of Calvin are known for their doctrinal feistiness. .

But it is not just the Reformed who like a good argument. Baptists are no less combative. It has been frequently observed that "an independent Baptist" is a redundancy. The noted New England Baptist leader Roger Williams saw such spiritual inadequacies in those around him that he could no longer share communion with anyone other than his wife—and then even she was suspect.

Suffice it to say that there is a spirit of competition and of needing to be right that infiltrates all of our denominations, businesses and institutions; it infiltrates all of us who seek to provide leadership within them. Spiritual formation in our inner world means we need to be pruned of our self-righteousness. One exhortation from the wisdom literature in the Old Testament that has helped me to desire pruning says, "Do not be too righteous; . . . why should you destroy yourself?" (Eccles 7:16). This is an instructive and thought-provoking verse.

Pruning of passion to maximize life. Another pruning I need is from a compulsive desire to be all I can be and to maximize my life. This may seem counterintuitive because as a leader I am challenged to maximize our financial situation and to run things as lean as possible. I like efficiencies and getting the most that I can out of money, time or even relationships. Sometimes I think this is good stewardship and defend it as such. I don't want to be sloppy with our resources. "Work; for the . . . night is coming" was not only a teaching of Jesus regarding spiritual readiness, but at times it has become a semi-conscious mantra leading to sheer addiction. I get angry at inefficiencies and am sad without new challenges. I understand in some small way the regret of Alexander the Great, who reportedly wept when he realized he had no more worlds to conquer.

Sometimes my instincts to "do it all" play out in family decisions, like loading up vacations with so much to do that they are
tiring rather than refreshing. Sometimes I try to maximize conference or meeting planning with too large an agenda or sessions
that are too long. (There seems to be a leadership axiom that the
kidney capacity of the person leading the meeting is far greater
than that of the meeting participants. The corollary is that when a
leader moves to being a participant, their kidney capacity de-
creases accordingly!)

I am also aware that when I do public speaking, I am inclined
to include far more material than what might be helpful to those
who are listening. As a leader I want to take advantage of every
opportunity to influence others, but sometimes this intensity can
actually distance me from those I want to lead. Quantity winds up
diminishing quality.

In response to these human propensities that they saw in themselves, Ignatius of Loyola and other spiritual leaders often speak
of the value of conscious detachment from those things that are
compulsive or disordered affections in our lives. Our compulsions
may start out as something good and even necessary, like eating
and drinking. But when we are consumed with eating or drinking
or sex or power, we become addicted to these behaviors and lose
the freedom of discernment as to what is healthy for us and for
others. As leaders we can also become addicted to efficiencies that
at first help our bottom line or our workload, but can become an
obsession that leaves out important relationships.

In response to this propensity to be efficient so I might maximize my life, I have found that the ancient practice of giving something up for the six-week period of Lent is a valuable annual discipline. For instance, I have regularly chosen to give up watching
all television during those weeks. This is not easy; I really enjoy
watching college basketball, and March madness always overlaps
some part of Lent.

But to be able to say no to watching hours of this basketball tournament has been spiritually energizing to me. It not only provides more discretionary hours for either rest or being with others, it gives me a pattern for making other choices of restraint. Choosing not to be consumed with efficiency is a great freedom that allows greater flexibility and spontaneity. As Jesus taught, it is not efficient to go after the one lost sheep at the expense of the other ninety-nine, but it is the right choice.

Pruning of soliciting praise. I am embarrassed to confess that I all too often solicit praise and recognition from others. This is probably connected again to that root sin of pride, but I find it especially debilitating in all forms of leadership. When I am under great work pressure, I long for others to say how well I am doing. But when I am brutally honest with myself, I am never completely satisfied and always look for more ways for others to notice what I have said or done.

One of the most common ways is to make sure that I get credit for my ideas. In a conversation, I may casually say, "in case you don't remember, I raised this issue several months ago"; or "I've been saying this for years." Sometimes this emphasis may be important if we have been ignored and we feel there is a need for a frank discussion of the issue. I don't think we should hide our light under a bushel. But more often than not, calling attention to our previous contributions can be a form of one-upmanship that is off-putting to others. When I find myself wanting more attention or recognition, it is a blaring reminder of my need for a greater awareness of God's grace in my life.

This grace manifests itself in at least two ways. One is a common grace that comes through the unsolicited praise from others. When this genuinely happens, I am less likely to try to need more. This is why healthy companies, universities and churches have a large measure of mutual encouragement, thanks and grace built into their cultures. When we are affirmed and appreciated on a regular basis by others, we don't need to do so much praising of ourselves. As we affirm and praise others, they too will be less needy of self-induced recognition. As St. Francis wrote in his famous prayer, "it is in giving that we receive" and this applies to words of praise and recognition.

But many of us may not have had such a family background or supportive working environment. Credit and recognition may always seem to be grabbed by the top person or the most vocal or the most powerful personality. Sometimes women or minorities or junior members of a team will feel that their contributions are lost until a more powerful or established leader says the same thing.

Or we may have a wonderfully supportive workplace with lots of "attaboy" and "go girl" encouragements. But even the positive words of others are not sufficient to meet the deepest needs that we have to be unconditionally accepted and loved. These needs can only be met by God. So when I am most desperate and tempted to do things so others will notice me, I find freedom in letting go of that need so that I can more fully receive God's grace.

I have even struggled with this in writing this book. Am I doing it for the recognition as an author and leader, or is it out of a sense of calling to share with others what God has given to me? Or is it both, in ways that are so woven together in my personality, family background and work experience that I can't pull them apart? I believe the latter is true, which is why I need the continual spiritual discernment and pruning of God in my life.

In accepting this need, I find it comforting that when Jesus taught his disciples about the necessity of spiritual pruning, he did so in the context of friendship and not of power. He said "I do not call you servants any longer, because the servant does not know what the master is doing; but I have called you friends, because I have made known to you everything that I have heard from the Father" (Jn 15:15). God's pruning of us does not come out of anger but out of love and self-revelation. He desires our friendship and our fruitfulness.

Maybe it is this recognition of the initiative and intentionality of God's horticultural activity in our lives that is part of the secret of spiritual formation. As long as we think we are doing the pruning based on our ability to be in control, we lose spiritual perspective and vitality. But when we are able to receive God's pruning of our compulsions, we are able to grow into all of our strength. Pruning is painful, and the issues for you may be different than mine, but as Walter Trobisch said, "Without pain, there is no growth."

THE DAILY EXAMEN

A classic spiritual discipline that I have found helpful in this pruning process is the daily examen. *Examen* comes from a Latin word referring to the weight indicator on a balance. Just as it takes some time for the swinging examen to settle after the weights are added, so it takes time for us to see where our lives are in balance or need some adjustment or pruning.

One way I have practiced this discipline is that before going to bed I think back over the day and ask two basic questions. The first question is, When did I have the greatest sense of God's presence in terms of the most joy or peace or other expressions of the fruit of the Spirit? Sometimes this is a conversation, while at other times it might be simply making a good decision. Usually though it is relational in nature. Recently I attended a baby shower for one of our employees, and as I looked around the room I had great delight in sensing God's creative activity in the people I work with. I find encouragement by reflecting on these expressions of God's presence.

The second question is, When did I feel very frustrated, dissatisfied or alone from God's Spirit? St. Ignatius referred to these negative thoughts and feelings as desolation. Again these are often related to relational matters, but underneath I frequently see the aberrant growth of my desire for praise or recognition or for wanting to do more in maximizing my life. However it is in these quiet moments at the end of the day that the pruning by God's Spirit gives me strength for the day to come.

THREE

A RENEWED MIND

The Practice of Humble Thought

There are many who seek knowledge for the
sake of knowledge: that is curiosity.
There are others who desire to know
in order that they may be known: this is vanity....
But there are those who seek knowledge
in order to edify others: that is love.

BERNARD OF CLAIRVAUX

The Pharisees were gathered around Jesus and a lawyer asked him what was the greatest commandment. Jesus knew it but he didn't quote it exactly the way it was written in Deuteronomy, where God told Israel through Moses to "love the LORD your God with all your heart, and with all your soul, and with all your might" (Deut 6:5). Jesus added the requirement "and with all your mind" (Lk 10:27). He interpreted this fundamental Old Testament teaching for his listeners in a way to make sure that they did not leave their minds out of their devotion to God.

Jesus' teaching on loving God with our minds has ironically become an inconvenient truth for many despite the historic witness and tremendous spiritual leadership of some great minds

like those of St. Augustine, St. Bonaventure and Jonathan Edwards. A brilliant and contemporary New Testament scholar in
his own right, Bishop N. T. Wright sees this reaction to the mind
as another battle in the cultural and spiritual war between ro-
manticism and rationalism. People react to what they perceive as
the tyranny of intellectual arrogance while others fight back
against what they perceive as emotional blackmail. It is another
expression of the leadership ellipse that needs strong focal points
of both heart and mind.

Today, though, as general interest in spirituality has increased,
there has been a concurrent spirit of benign neglect if not antago-
nism toward the spiritual role of the mind in various religious
teachings. This is also true among Christians who have rightly
reacted to sterile formulations of faith and doctrine that have
squelched rather than aided their longings for God. Idolatry of our
rationality has prompted some to see the mind as a barrier rather
than a means to a deeper spiritual life.

As an example of this, I was sitting in a circle in a retreat center
with about twenty other Christian leaders who were interested in
pursuing a deeper spiritual life. The topic for the evening discussion was on the role of the mind in spiritual formation. I was very
interested in this topic because the life of the mind has played a
big and conscious part in my life.

I am a Myers-Briggs "T," which means that my thinking is a
major strength. I was trained as an engineer; I always did well in
math. I love to conceptualize, to strategize, to plan and organize.
I love to read and think. Suffice it to say that I fit a stereotypical
mold of a highly cognitive person (which sounds much better than
nerd).

So I was encouraged when the presenter began his time that
night by referring to the apostle Paul's familiar exhortation to "be
transformed by the renewing of your minds" (Rom 12:2). I was
eager for more insight into this dynamic of transformation by

mental renewal. Thus I was surprised when he reversed this cause and effect relationship, and said that spiritual transformation is what renews the mind and not the other way around. This did not seem to be a logical interpretation of the text.

But this was not the only time I had been challenged with whether my mind was an asset or a liability with respect to spiritual growth. I had read a series of articles by Henri Nouwen in *Sojourners* magazine titled "Descend with the Mind into the Heart." I was tremendously impressed with what he wrote and the integrity with which he wrote it. At the time, Nouwen was teaching pastoral theology at Yale before he later moved to teach at Harvard. Subsequently he left the academic world to be involved with the L'Arche community, which cares for the disabled in Toronto. There was no question for me about Nouwen's devotion to God or brilliance of mind.

However, the discomfort that I faced was that the title of these articles seemed to imply if not overtly teach that the mind was inferior to the heart; or that the mind was some type of superficial, preliminary pathway to the real and deeper spirituality of the heart. This didn't seem to measure up to my understanding of the Scriptures that taught that the heart (not the mind) is what is "desperately wicked and deceitful above all things." Nor did it help me to love God with all of my mind.

Yet, I took Nouwen seriously and listened carefully to what he said. In doing so I discovered that the formulation of the phrase "descend with the mind into the heart" was not originally from Nouwen but from the nineteenth-century Russian mystic Theophan the Recluse—whose name gives a clue that he was not in business meetings all day!

Furthermore, the idea or conviction for this spirituality went back to the desert fathers and mothers of fourth-century Egypt. These saints, who fled into the wilderness to escape the rampant carnality of their culture, were not consciously trying to integrate their life with the demands of technology and cultural expectations. In fact according to the twentieth-century monastic leader Thomas Merton, the desert fathers "saw society as a shipwreck from which every single individual had to swim for his life." Quite an interesting metaphor for a desert life.

So I was not sure that either Theophan or the desert fathers or this speaker had much to say to me about how to use my mind to deepen my spirituality in twenty-first-century life. I didn't feel called to either leave my life or in some way negate it. I was willing to learn from the desert fathers, but I didn't want to become one. Instead I wanted to learn what Paul meant about being transformed by the renewal of my mind.

A NONCONFORMED MIND

The prerequisite for mental renewal for Paul is his warning not "to be conformed to this world [or to this age]." Throughout the history of the church this exhortation has been interpreted to avoid "worldly" activities, however they might be culturally defined. The stereotype of this approach is reflected in the old fundamentalist doggerel "I don't swear, dance or chew, or go out with any boys that do."

Although such a statement may either make us laugh or cry, the mature Christian life is nevertheless characterized by disciplined choices about what is and is not good to do, and that these choices are connected to the mind. At the very beginning of Romans, Paul observes that those who have rejected God have done so by suppressing the truth about God. He says that although they knew God, "they became futile in their thinking, and their senseless minds were darkened." The result of such aberrant thinking was that they were "filled with every kind of wickedness" (Rom 1:21, 29).

Paul's witness is striking as it relates to our decision-making processes. As a theological crime-scene investigator, he not only makes the accusations against aberrant and immoral behavior but goes back to trace the culprit for it. And the primary reason he gives for acting wrongly is thinking wrongly, especially thinking wrongly about God. When we don't acknowledge and worship God as Creator, we not only become futile in our thinking but our hearts and instinctual gut behaviors become impure.

A good example of this is thinking that God must always choose to bless us with success—from finding good parking spots to achieving all of our goals. When we think this way, we become enamored and driven by success as an indication of our faithfulness and a mark of God's blessing. Unfortunately and mysteriously, we are not always successful, and our external success is not always directly associated with our faithfulness.

We see this in dramatic fashion in Hebrews 11, which catalogs the great "heroes of faith." Some of these Old Testament saints, like Enoch and Abraham, cross the finish line of their earthly experience with success, while others experience great human failures, even to the extent of being "sawn in two." Even Moses, the one who met with God face to face, ended his earthly life with the disappointment of not being allowed to cross into the Promised Land despite more than forty years of blood, sweat and tears in his leadership.

Another biblical teaching on nonconformity comes from the Psalter. Psalm 1 celebrates the nonconformist who does not follow the counsel of the "wicked" and who delights in the "law of the Lord." One of the synonyms for the wicked in the first verse Psalm 1 is "scoffer," or one who mocks or makes light of God's instructions. The clear teaching of the psalm is that the happy or blessed or righteous person is the one who does not imbibe or delight in these profane influences. Although we cannot be isolated or ignorant of such wickedness, it is spiritually debilitating to embrace or promote it. Caustic language, arrogance toward God and immoral behavior are characteristics of spiritual instability and chaff. Ridicule is never a replacement for righteousness.

Instead, a blessed person is one who is delighted and immersed in the teachings of the Lord. Such a person is consciously choosing to have a right relationship with God and consequently exhibits a life of fruitfulness and spiritual prosperity. We use our minds to choose whom we follow, what we read, whose advice we accept, whose lifestyles we emulate. We choose with our minds whether to know God's teachings and whether to obey them. What we think directly affects what we feel and what we do.

Practically speaking, I find that paying attention to what I am thinking about in my unscripted moments is often revealing as to what is important to me. I first became aware of this when I was doing an undergraduate thesis in materials science at Drexel University. My thesis adviser was Dr. Richard Heckel. Living out the humorous association of his name, Dr. Heckel used to challenge our class that unless we were thinking about our thesis when we woke up every morning, we weren't thinking about it seriously enough.

So listening to my unguarded thoughts is a valuable diagnostic practice to discern what is going on inside of me. When my waking moments are focused on how others view me or on my negative thoughts about them, I am not being renewed. I am living in conformity to the world's values of status and power.

By way of contrast, Paul encourages the Philippian believers to think about whatever is true, honorable, just, pure, pleasing, commendable and worthy of praise (Phil 4:8). This is not just positive thinking or temperamental upbeatness, but a genuine honoring of God and others. It is characteristic of a renewed mind that is not conformed to the world.

A SPIRITUAL MIND

Renewing our minds is not just resisting evil influences; it is also pursuing and receiving the quiet work of God's Spirit in the warp and woof our lives. Alice and I have a lovely deck on the back of our house. Some of this book has been conceived sitting in a lounge chair (with our dog) amidst dozens of beautiful flowering plants while watching birds vying for the best perches on our bird feeders. One of the birds we most enjoy watching is the goldfinch. The males in full plumage have a brilliant yellow breast, and they fly like they are on a roller coaster. They are fun and beautiful to watch.

One spring, several years ago, Alice was watching a goldfinch couple that kept coming to our finch feeder. She noticed that the male did not start out to be so brightly yellow but was more of a dull tan. However, as the weather got warmer, the gold got more pronounced—without the goldfinch doing anything special beyond just being a goldfinch.

For Alice this goldfinch became a metaphor of the work of God in her life as she simply lived as she was created to be. It reminded her of what Paul wrote to the Corinthian church of "being transformed . . . from one degree of glory to another" (2 Cor 3:18). Just going about our daily pattern of life can be a transforming experience in the hands of God. His grace is the necessary foundation and framework for our lives and minds to be renewed.

But if we are the created and not the Creator, and God is doing this work in us, what is our role in responding to this divine initiative? What does a spiritual mind look like? How do we set our minds on the Spirit instead of the flesh? Paul helps us to answer these questions when he tells the church at Ephesus that they should not live "in the futility of their minds" but "be renewed in the spirit of your minds," and then lists what that means (see Ephesians 4).

First of all they should put away falsehood and "speak the truth to our neighbors." A spiritual mind is one that rejects all forms of deceit such as pretense, exaggeration, misinformation and lying. Rather it is in tune with truth telling. Paul even allows that we can be angry in our truth telling if we do not allow our

anger to become sin by nursing it overnight. Such high standards of honesty are not easy for anyone to reach all of the time,
especially leaders. We feel the pressure to make ourselves look
good and are always communicating to our "neighbors" at work
about what is being done and said in our jobs. But truthfulness
is at the heart of our integrity.

Another mark of the spiritual mind is how we speak to and about
each other. Instead of responding to our colleagues with anger,
wrangling, slander or malice, Paul says we are to be kind to one
another, tenderhearted and forgiving to one another. This too is not
easy because we may not want to lead that way. Such a style may be
perceived as weak or may threaten our patterns of success. Bishop
N. T. Wright tells the story of the scholar who wrote scathing reviews of his colleagues' work, but then started attending conferences where he met the people he was reviewing and discovered he
really liked them—so he stopped going to the conferences!

A Prayerful Mind

What has been most helpful to me in trying to develop a spiritual
mind is to specifically pray my frustrations and tensions with colleagues to the Lord. I remember in one extended series of events,
I was continually getting into conflict with another leader. Although we liked each other, our temperaments and leadership
styles were very different. What seemed right to me felt like judg-
ment to him, and his initiatives always seemed to be undermining
my spheres of responsibilities. We tried to work things through
but we kept irritating and arguing with each other.

But then I started to pray my frustrations and my own feelings
of inadequacy to the Lord. I prayed for patience and understanding of my colleague rather than for victory or resolution. This led
me to pray for more self-understanding and patience with myself
as well. Talking with God about what I couldn't fix was wonderfully releasing. Over time I was able to not only enjoy his differ-

ences but to solicit them as well. He too found a greater freedom in asking for my perspectives.

I learned from this that it doesn't work to deny negative feelings that inevitably occur in leadership. I am a sinner and I work with sinners, so we are sure to sin against each other. It should not be a surprise then when others disappoint us or we disappoint them.

Suppressing these inevitable feelings does not help us live with integrity. The feelings do not go away but will pop up later, even in a different context. Sometimes we send or receive hurtful emotional messages that were really intended for someone else. Long-term, unacknowledged and unexpressed feelings become a time bomb waiting to explode under the stresses and pressures of organizational life.

So when I experience an inappropriate action or display of anger in either myself or in others, I choose to think and pray that perhaps there is something else going on beyond the immediate situation. There may be long-standing issues from family of origin or immediate family difficulties or a personal struggle with sin.

The immediate issues prompting the anger do need to be addressed, but praying for the person and myself is spiritually and practically redemptive. In a real and deeply spiritual way, instead of letting my heart and feelings control my actions, I need to raise my heart to my mind and let a prayerful mind tutor my heart as to how best to respond to interpersonal difficulties.

I find the example of Moses with Miriam to be insightful in this regard. Moses had married a dark-skinned Cushite woman, Zipporah. Miriam and Aaron responded to Moses' interracial marriage by speaking against him to others and thus starting a palace coup. They said, "Has the LORD spoken only through Moses? Has he not spoken through us also?" (Num 12:2).

This verbal insurrection displeased God, who was so angry with them that Miriam became leprous and Aaron became petrified. And here is where Moses' leadership shines the strongest.

Instead of letting any feelings of betrayal govern his actions and allowing Miriam to live with her punishment of leprosy, Moses prays to the Lord, "O God, please heal her" (Num 12:13). Somehow, Moses had the discernment and the security to want a healed Miriam rather than a bitter, diseased woman around him. He prayed rather than schemed.

The second reason to pray my grievances is that I know from the remarkably candid admissions of the psalmists, like the complaint against those "who hate me without reason," that I can trust God to hear my negative thoughts. They do not take him unawares or invalidate our prayer communication. In fact they deepen it and provide the spiritual resources to subsequently pursue honest discussions with our colleagues.

I don't believe that Christian spirituality should lead either to conflict or be conflict avoidant, but it should rather promote conflict resolution that is prayerful and not just procedural. Paul tells the Corinthian believers that it is not only valuable to pray with the Spirit in a sense of devotional ecstasy but also to "pray with the mind" (1 Cor 14:15). A spiritual mind is one that uses our cognitive abilities in prayer to help work through our relational struggles and difficulties.

A PREPARED MIND

Another dimension to mental renewal comes from the apostle Peter. Although he was a fisherman in contrast to the scholarly Paul, he too wrote about the importance of the mind. In his first letter to Christians scattered by persecution he uses the pithy instruction, "Prepare your minds for action" (1 Pet 1:13). This statement has a rich biblical context.

The exhortation to prepare goes back to the night of the first Passover, when instructions were given to the Israelites to get ready to move out. They were told to "gird up their loins" which meant to pull up their flowing robes so that they would be able to move quickly and run without tripping. They were to be ready to leave Egypt quickly with their sandals on, their staff in hand and their loins girded.

Peter uses this phrase with respect to the mind. The King James Version translated his words to "gird up the loins of your mind" for action. They were not to be intellectually lazy but prepared for serious thinking. Later, in the third chapter of his letter, Peter tells his readers to "always be ready to make your defense to anyone who demands from you an accounting for the hope that is in you." The world then and now is not shy in challenging us to give reasons for what we believe, and they are quick to notice any shallowness or hypocrisy in how we respond.

Unfortunately, we are not always so well prepared. In 1994 the noted evangelical historian Mark Noll wrote *The Scandal of the Evangelical Mind* in which he boldly stated "there is not much of an evangelical mind." Although there has been a marked increase in significant Christian scholarship in the academy in the years since then, there is often an intellectual flabbiness and shallowness in the church and in the marketplace among many Christians, whether evangelical or not. Not only professors should know biblical ethics but also business and professional leaders in all fields of endeavor.

Intellectual laziness not only affects our reputation and influence in the world, but it also affects our spiritual life. J. P. Moreland writes that "the contemporary Christian mind is starved and as a result we have impoverished souls." The late Pope John Paul II put the situation both broadly and pointedly, saying, "We need spiritual values. We need a revolution of the mind." Neither Peter nor John Paul II was talking about mere intellectual firepower. They were talking about a thoughtful and active Christian faith— minds prepared for action.

I like the story told by historian Patrick Henry about his mother-in-law, who instead of praying "make us ever mindful of the needs of others" prayed "make us ever needful of the minds of others." Although both petitions are good, the mistaken prayer expresses a keen insight into the learning process. We do need the minds of others to prepare our own minds.

To do this, we need to protect our time for serious reading. This is becoming more difficult to do in an electronic age that saps our discretionary time with constant e-mails, text messaging, sports updates and phone calls. But we need to take time to read authors that can both nurture our souls and prepare our minds for action. Such reading takes focused time and reflective thought. Outstanding leadership usually requires outstanding readership.

A major consequence of a mind prepared for action is a mind that does battle with worldly wisdom. Going back to Paul, we hear him challenging the Corinthian Christians to "take every thought captive to obey Christ" (2 Cor 10:5). Another way of stating this perspective came many centuries later. Dutch politician and theologian Abraham Kuyper powerfully declared "in the total expanse of human life there is not one single square inch of which the Christ, who alone is sovereign, does not declare, 'That is mine!' " A prepared mind is actively involved in this great intellectual reclamation project for the sake of Jesus Christ.

Consider an example from the world of music: one of the greatest and best-known pieces of music in the Western world is Beethoven's Ninth Symphony and its stirring choral climax, "Ode to Joy." Many church hymnals include this hymn, and the movie *Beethoven's Scribe* gives a dramatic rendition of the power of this piece. Unfortunately, the words to this hymn are not particularly Christian and could even be described as pagan. According to Beethoven, worship and praise were an "ode to joy" rather than to the God of the universe. By way of contrast let me quote David Clowney's rich theological hymn "God All Nature Sings Thy Glory," which was written for Beethoven's same stirring music. (It is interesting to note that he wrote this while in high school.)

> God, all nature sings Thy glory, and Thy works proclaim
> Thy might;
> Ordered vastness in the heavens, Ordered course of day
> and night.
> Beauty in the changing seasons, Beauty in the morning sea;
> All the changing moods of nature, Praise the changeless
> Trinity.

> Clearer still we see Thy hand in Man whom Thou hast
> made for Thee.
> Ruler of creation's glory, Image of Thy Majesty.
> Music, art, the fruitful garden, All the labor of his days,
> Are the calling of his Maker, To the harvest feast of praise.

> But our sins have spoiled Thy image; Nature conscience
> only serve
> As unceasing, grim reminders, Of the wrath which we
> deserve.
> Yet Thy grace and saving mercy, In Thy Word of truth
> revealed
> Claim the praise of all who know Thee, In the blood of
> Jesus sealed.

> God of glory, power and mercy, All creation praises Thee;
> We, Thy creatures, would adore Thee, Now and through
> eternity.
> Saved to magnify thy goodness, Grant us strength to do
> Thy will;
> With our acts as with our voices, Thy commandments to
> fulfill.

This hymn made such an impression on us that Alice and I wrote our own verse based on Psalm 100 to be sung at our wedding to this grand melody.

Joyful, joyful we adore thee, King of Kings and Lord of
       Lords,
Come into his gates with singing, know ye that the Lord is
       God.
He hath made us. We are his children.
Joy and praise to him we bring.
Thank him for his loving kindness, Thank God for our life
       in him.

Taking captive thoughts and making them obedient to Christ is
a redemptive process. It is not just baptizing secular thoughts with
Christian language but is taking expressions of truth and shaping
them into the purposes of God and for the glory of God. It is not a
Christian veneer but a Christian vision of discipleship that follows Jesus as Savior and Lord in how and what we think.

A Christian mind does not even have to have Christian language to honor God. Jesus' proverbial lily of the field does not
have a proof text tied to its stem, yet it glorifies God by being what
it was created to be. Having a prepared mind implies that we are
equipped to reflect God's glory in our thinking and in the use of
our minds. Vigorous and rigorous thinking are part of the calling
to Christian leaders.

An example of a leader with a prepared mind that I have had
the privilege of knowing is Dr. Timothy Johnson, noted medical
correspondent for ABC News. Tim wrote a book called *Finding
God in the Questions* that made it to the *New York Times* Best Seller
list. Tim's book was not a solutions manual but a testimonial of his
search for finding God in the context of his medical and scientific
discipline. Tim looked face to face with the difficult questions of
undeserved suffering in the world and why it matters to be a follower of Jesus in such a world.

Shortly before his book was published he gave a copy to Peter
Jennings, the late, celebrated news anchor of ABC News. Jennings

was very skeptical although he was interested in matters of faith. As he later shared publicly, he encouraged Tim not to publish his book because he feared that Tim would lose his reputation for objectivity if he went public with such a strong expression of Christian faith.

However, as Jennings again related, the morning the book was released he read a review of it in the *Wall Street Journal* that was very positive. Later that evening at a reception for Tim, Peter admitted he was wrong about the book and he and other ABC colleagues spoke glowingly about Tim's integrity as a scientist and as a dedicated follower of Jesus. Tim's mind was prepared for action in the intense environment of network news.

A HUMBLE MIND

Perhaps the best indicator of a renewed mind is that of a humble mind. The apostle Peter writes to his followers, "Finally, all of you, have unity of spirit, sympathy, love for one another, a tender heart, and a humble mind" (1 Pet 3:8).

Every year our leadership team has an annual three-day retreat in the early fall and a one-day retreat in the winter. Usually I will choose a theme text for our times together, and frequently I have chosen this teaching of Peter. It is a great context for how teams should work together. I don't use it to beat down hard discussion but rather use it as an invitation for deeper spiritual sensitivities that enable vigorous and difficult discussions. A key component for this to happen, though, is a humble mind.

A humble mind might sound like an oxymoron because we may be more used to intellectual arrogance or argumentation. We may be guilty of this ourselves or see it clearly in others. Humility is also a difficult virtue to think about. Once we are conscious of it, we are in danger of losing it. How de we pursue humility with humility. How do we follow Peter's exhortation to have a humble mind?

I find encouragement in the life of the Old Testament prophet Daniel. He is a great example for not only Sunday school lessons but everyone working in a leadership environment. Although Daniel was a prisoner of war, taken captive by the Babylonians, he was faithful to his God *and* to his successive pagan employers, Kings Nebuchadnezzar, Belshazzar and Darius. He became the ruler over the province of Babylon and the chief counselor for the king without compromising his Jewish dietary restrictions or his patterns of prayer.

Near the end of Daniel's life we gain some insight into how and why God used him so significantly in such hallways of influence. An angel appeared to Daniel and reminded him that since the first day "you set your mind to gain understanding and to humble yourself before your God" (Dan 10:12). Even the English word *understanding* communicates humility as it literally means "standing under." Daniel approached his governmental jobs with humility and used his mind in a humble way that led to great success.

But he did not use his position for his own glory. He continually gave credit to God. He was honored and respected through three regimes, but without moral compromise or self-promotion. He even was an effective evangelistic witness to King Nebuchadnezzar, who made this remarkable statement about Daniel's god.

> How great are his signs,
> how mighty his wonders!
> His kingdom is an everlasting kingdom,
> and his sovereignty is from generation to generation.
> (Dan 4:3)

All of this was a result of Daniel setting his mind to gain understanding and humbling himself before God.

However, the greatest and perfect example of humility is that of Jesus. Before Jesus met with his disciples for the Last Supper, John records that "Jesus, knowing that the Father had given all things into his hands, and that he had come from God and was going to God, got up from the table, took off his outer robe, and tied a towel around himself . . . and began to wash the disciples' feet" (Jn 13:3-5). Here we see the epitome of humility, the leader, teacher and Lord, stooping to do the menial task of foot washing.

But Jesus' willingness to "get down and dirty" was prefaced by an accurate self-knowledge of whom he was and where he was called to go. Jesus was not acting in a self-effacing, "I'm not worthy" kind of false humility. He was acting from strength of self-awareness, and it led directly to serving the disciples.

In other words, a humble mind is not an ignorant mind but a mind that is used for the sake of others. Paul states this most dramatically when he wrote to the Philippians that we should "let the same mind be in you that was in Christ Jesus" (Phil 2:5). In what became an elegant hymn of the early church, Paul describes the mind of Christ, who

> did not regard equality with God
> as something to be exploited,
> but emptied himself,
> taking the form of a slave,
> being born in human likeness. (Phil 2:6-7)

A humble mind is not a disembodied mind. It is not a heavenly mind without earthly good. Rather, it seeks knowledge in order to love and serve others. In this regard, I think of my wife's brother-in-law, John Stanford. He was trained as a solid-state physicist and was on the faculty of Iowa State University for many years. However he became intrigued with the work of George Washington Carver, a graduate of Iowa State and the noted African American researcher who was able to show the multiple uses and value of peanuts.

Largely through the example of George Washington Carver, John decided to see how his own research could be of practical help to common people. This conviction led him to the study of tornadoes. He became an expert on tornadoes and atmospheric physics, and was able to help people better prepare for and protect themselves from twisters. Not every field of endeavor has this same kind of option for practical application, but all of our jobs have opportunities to love and serve others with a humble mind.

DESCENT *WITH* THE MIND

Theophan the Recluse wrote about "descending with the mind into the heart." Maybe he got it right after all. Upon reflection, I realized he didn't say "descend from the mind into the heart" suggesting that the mind should be left behind in our spiritual journey. Rather he said we should "descend *with* the mind." The mind is to be our companion along the way. As I seek to move from my external appearances into a greater inner awareness, I need my mind to go with me on this journey. I need my heart to be tutored with biblical truth and I need a spiritual and prepared mind to lead me into holy nonconformity. Ultimately, I need to be transformed by a renewed and prayerful mind that is characterized by humble thought.

A Dancing Heart

The Practice of Involvement

Activity precedes contemplation, but contemplation
must be expressed in service to one's neighbor.

GREGORY THE GREAT

One Sunday morning our church had a commissioning service for a group going to one of the poorest places in the country, Cohoma, Mississippi, to help build houses with Habitat for Humanity. As I sat in the pew and listened, in the words of John Wesley, "My heart was strangely warmed" to the idea of joining the others on this trip. I had the flexibility of taking a vacation week, and after church I called the associate pastor who was leading the group. He wasn't sure there was room but he said he would get back to me in several days.

As I waited for his answer, I had an increasing uncertainty about whether I really wanted to do this. I had great respect for Habit for Humanity, but this endeavor was very much out of my comfort zone. I am not a handy man. I was trained as an engineer but am much better with doing equations than putting up Sheetrock.

I also don't like hot weather and the projected temperatures for the Mississippi Delta region were in the high 90s, with high humidity. Furthermore, the prospect of a long drive in a van with people I didn't know, followed by sleeping in an un-air-conditioned church all-purpose room for a week was not all that attractive either.

But deep down my greatest fear was that I would not be in a leadership role. I wouldn't have my status and ability to control or avoid things I may not have liked. I would be learning just by being part of a team in doing something I wasn't very good at. So when I heard that there was room for me on the team, I did some real soul-searching.

On the surface, I wanted to back out. This would not be an efficient use of my time. Vacation was supposed to be relaxing, not work. But my deeper longings to be more in touch with the purposes of God prompted me to go ahead.

That week turned out to be one of the best weeks of my life. I found that there was a great liberation to not always being in charge or responsible for something. I discovered many new and much younger friends who have continued to be good friends even though we now live in different states. I learned firsthand of the devastating effects of poverty, of alcoholism and racism. I met folks who had a buoyant faith in God despite their circumstances, and I also learned a little bit about building houses! That project was a dancing-heart experience as it led me to be meaningfully involved with others.

Experiences like this don't automatically happen in leadership, because unless we work for a ministry like Habitat they are not usually a strategic priority for getting our particular job done. Furthermore leadership often implies organizing and getting others to do such work. Good leadership holds people accountable and is structured rather than spontaneous.

Yet when we overly protect ourselves and don't allow ourselves freedom to be involved with others, we lose a spiritual edge of being led by God beyond our known plans. We also miss out on the joy of working with others. This is where our inner life directly affects our disposition to be responsively involved with others. It helps us to be servants.

CONTEMPLATION AND ACTION

For about twelve years I had a good friend, Koichi Ottawa, in Japan. Although we don't see each other now because of distance and job changes, for that period of time we did see each other every several years at international conferences. During those times together, we would always find some time to get away from the meetings and talk about our families, our jobs and how we were doing in juggling all of our personal and leadership responsibilities.

Ottawa spoke with a heavy Japanese accent and felt shy about his imperfect English (that was far better than my nonexistent Japanese). However, he did understand puns, and his keen sense of humor often surprised me with his play on English words. One such occasion was when we were talking about the significance of spiritual formation for leaders. I was lamenting that sometimes I did not see the connection between taking the time to focus inwardly when there were so many things to do outwardly. I was fighting with my need to get things done.

Ottawa smiled at me and said that being in the "presence" of God was necessary for me being a "presents" for others. At first I didn't get it, and I wanted to correct his wrong use of the plural. But then it dawned on me that what Ottawa was cleverly saying was that there is a strong connection between being with God and the ability to do things and be a gift for others. My leadership ellipse was not two separate worlds that didn't inform each other. Rather, how I lead is shaped by whom I am.

I later learned that this was not a new insight into the understanding of spirituality and leadership. In the late sixth century, and against his own desires, a monk by the name of Gregory was chosen to be pope. Although he was far more secure with the private life of study and prayer, he was immediately catapulted into not only a position of structural leadership in the church but he also became the primary civil authority in charge of an army at war and in coping with years of famine and social chaos in Rome.

In struggling with this inner-outer time conflict, Gregory wrote "While my mind obliged me to serve this present world in outward action, its cares began to threaten me so that I was in danger of being engulfed in it not only in outward action, but what is more serious, in my mind." Consequently he learned sometimes to "turn away from the distractions of knowing about things to the serious, even frightening, task of reflection on the inner self."

Chris Armstrong writes that despite Gregory's continuous struggle between work and prayer, "he was able to formulate a pattern of spiritual renewal in the midst of busyness and spiritual leadership amid secular demands." This was at least one reason he was designated "Gregory the Great."

Today, the popular Franciscan retreat leader Richard Rohr has a center for "action and contemplation." The interdenominational community of Taizé, France, began with the vision of a Presbyterian pastor for a place of worship and reconciliation. He protected Jewish war refugees in World War II and then later cared for German prisoners of war. Now more than one hundred thousand people each year flock to this community centered on worship, prayer and Bible study. At the same time, the community sends out people to serve the poor in more than fifty countries. The Taizé community lives a synergistic life of inner and outer spiritual health.

But the importance of this direct relationship between pietism and practice is not intuitively obvious in our make-it-happen culture.

MAKE IT HAPPEN CULTURE
In our democratic, capitalistic nation there is a dominant story line that not only can we be all we want to be but we can accom-

plish anything we want to do. Although there are still many places of both overt and unconscious racism and sexism, the American dream of unlimited personal achievement is alive and well. As the campaign slogan for President Barack Obama boldly stated, "Yes We Can."

This way of thinking and acting has been the tremendous engine of accomplishment in not only business but also in academic research, in sports and even Christian ministries. Church growth itself has been fueled in part through the phenomenal explosion of parachurch ministries in the second half of the twentieth century. Entrepreneurial leaders with highly focused visions and strong business practices were able to not only effectively pursue their missions but contributed their successful practices of evangelism, Bible study, social justice and missionary outreach to the church. I heard of one Catholic leader who encouraged a young priest of a dying parish to hire an evangelical on his staff because evangelicals know how to make churches grow.

However, I also overheard a noted evangelical leader giving a series of directions to his staff with the final exhortation to "make it happen." I remember being initially impressed with this leader's confidence and strength of leadership. He was not going to be satisfied with excuses of why something did not work. I knew that in many Christian contexts and often in the academic world there is a bias against action because of a fear of failure. Even the business world experiences lethargic responses to taking necessary action. "Just don't stand there, do something" is a common cry of exasperation among leaders in almost all spheres of work.

But upon reflection, that specific directive of "make it happen" did not ring true from a spiritual perspective. It felt like a command that was laced with unhealthy bits of ego, control and power. I found myself being both attracted to this leader's gifts and also being somewhat repulsed by how he was using them. There was more hubris than humility. There was a sense that we really can control our lives and the lives of others on our own strength without a sense of dependence on God. Such a perspective is what Parker Palmer refers to as "functional atheism," and this is a problem for us when we either want or feel pressured to make a decision to show we are in charge. We don't take time to pray or wait for a clearer sense of what might be best.

Yet, although I cringed at what felt like a spiritual machismo, I also didn't like the bumper-sticker theology of "Let go and let God." That too seemed like a cop-out from serious Christian responsibility. In fact, someone gave me a copy of François Fénelon's classic book *Letting Go*, and I just couldn't read it at the time because the premise seemed contrary to biblical teachings like the Great Commission and the Great Commandments, which call for a more active faith. I affirmed the substance of the cliché that God created us as human beings and not human doings, but I also believed the New Testament teaching that faith without works is dead. I struggled with how to connect an internal life of quiet with an active external life of leadership and service. What I really wanted was a way for my inner life to clearly shape my outer life rather than being separated from it.

THE POWER OF OUR AFFECTIONS

Since then I have discovered at deeper and deeper levels the fundamental driving force of my affections for how I live my life. I am learning that although there is unquestionable value in having a quiet heart that is still before God, my spiritual calling is not passivity. A quiet heart provides the environment in which I can pay better attention to the promptings of God, but my life is not to be a void from actively knowing God in the world.

For me, marriage has been a valuable metaphor for understanding the necessary and changing amplitude of my relationship with God. Scripture speaks of our relationship with God as being a marriage, perhaps because marriage is not only a universal institution but is also our most intimate human experience. In our marriage Alice and I richly enjoy our times of quietly reading or walking together. But our marriage is also alive with engaged communication and what we do together. It is our love that binds us together rather than any specific activity pattern or lack thereof.

So it seems to be in our relationship with God. It is our affections that either push us closer to God or pull us further from God. In *A Treatise Concerning Religious Affections*, Jonathan Edwards delineates between false affections and true religion, which "consists of holy affections" that incline our heart toward God. Edwards further believed that love was the master affection and was the true test of our spirituality.

In a totally different context but with a similar conclusion, Bill Cosby was once asked how to keep teens from killing each other for their sneakers. He succinctly responded, "Change their desires." We don't literally kill each other, but if you are like me, we as leaders are regularly tempted to construct murderous comments about others to gain or protect our reputation. We may be disciplined enough not to say what we are thinking and feeling, but unless our desires and affections are changed to fully resist these temptations our leadership will be tainted by an underlying self-centeredness. Our internal affections are a tremendous driving force in who we are and how we lead. They give shape to our leadership ellipse.

A Dancing Heart

The title of this chapter begins with "A Dancing Heart." Despite my lack of dancing ability, I love the way this image connects soul and body. I enjoy watching people do classic and traditional dances. Their bodies are in tune with their emotions. Their faces are alive and there is energy in their feet.

Spiritually, our bodies and our souls are intertwined as well. We see this in Scripture. When Elizabeth and Mary met to share

their pregnancies, John the Baptist "leaped for joy" in the womb of
Elizabeth at the greeting of Mary (Lk 1:41). When the handicapped
beggar was healed at the temple in Jerusalem, he entered the temple "walking and leaping and praising God" (Acts 3:8). Enthusias-
tic physical response is a natural response of being in the presence
of God.

Dancing also reflects a balance of freedom and discipline. Robert Capon in his delightful book *Bed and Board* describes the difference between a dance and a march. He says "In a parade, really
unequal beings are dressed alike, given guns of identical length,
trained to hold them at the same angle, and ordered to keep step
with a fixed beat. But it is not the parade that is true to life; it is
the dance. . . . Nothing is less personal than a parade; nothing
more so than a dance." There is a freedom to the dance; there is
weariness with marching.

Applying this to the spiritual life, I desire to dance and not just
march. Currently Christians from various denominational backgrounds are rediscovering spiritual disciplines. Disciplines are
indeed necessary for meaningful growth in the Christian life, just
as they are in other parts of life like athletics, medicine and music.
The famed Polish pianist Paderewski is reported to have said, "If I
miss one day of practice, I notice it. If I miss two days, the critics
notice it. If I miss three days, the audience notices it." Even the
categories of learning in the university world are referred to as
disciplines, which imply certain standards of professional rigor.

In spiritual formation, though, the emphasis is not primarily
on achieving a professional competence measured by external
standards, such as how much time we spend in prayer or how
often we fast. Rather, spiritual disciplines are a means to an end of
glorifying God in the freedom of his Spirit. They help shape the
path to spiritual maturity, but they are not the goal. Even the role
of a "spiritual director" is not to give advice or direction per se, but
to be a companion along the journey or to be a midwife to what is

being spiritually born in the person seeking spiritual guidance.

When I was growing up I took piano lessons from a dapper Englishman, Mr. Milligan, who came to our home once a week. As a young boy who liked excitement and baseball (not that they are mutually exclusive!) I labored to learn my scales and exercises. The only way I could at first endure them was to try to play them faster or louder. But what Mr. Milligan wanted most was for me to play them accurately.

Gradually I learned that training and strengthening my fingers by these repetitive requirements was preparing me for playing music. At the end of every one of my piano lessons, Mr. Milligan would sit down at the piano and play a beautiful piece of music that without words told me what disciplined practice might accomplish.

In another time of my boyhood, my love for baseball won out over being a musician. My mom figured this out when I was trying to play the violin. She came into a quiet living room where I was supposed to be practicing, only to find me swinging my violin bow like a baseball bat at some wads of paper I had rolled up.

But these lessons from my failed musical career help me understand some of the dynamics of spiritual growth. I need the disciplines to give me focus, but my aspiration is for a spiritual aesthetic that is beautiful to both me and to others. I don't want to be on the stage of leadership and just play scales that may be accurate but uninspiring to others. So how do we develop good internal disciplines that liberate us to dance in our leadership?

Listening to God. A prerequisite for good dancing is the ability to hear the music. The music gives structure, form and boundaries while also quickening the spirit. It sets the beat while stirring the emotions. We listen attentively to the music if we want to be inspired to dance well. A dancing heart for God is dependent on a heart listening to God.

The testimony of many Christian leaders throughout the ages is that the best way to hear God is through what we commonly refer to as a devotional or "quiet time." These daily opportunities to listen to God through Scripture and prayer are often directed by others through a liturgical guide like Phyllis Tickle's *The Divine Hours* or through devotional Bible study guides. It seems that even this small act of submission to the spiritual guidance in these resources is valuable in preparing us to hear and receive from the Lord beyond our own anxious thoughts.

As a growing Christian in college I used a series of Bible study guides that directed me to specific Bible passages with a series of questions for reflection and application. My devotional habits changed though when Alice and I met and got married. She was using a resource called *Encounter with God* published by Scripture Union. The strength of this resource is that it leads the user through reading the whole Bible over a period of four years with some reflective and insightful comments for each reading.

Another valuable spiritual exercise in hearing from God through Scripture is referred to as "lectio divina" or divine reading. There are many books such as *Spiritual Disciplines Handbook* by Adele Calhoun that describe this practice in greater detail, but basically it is a way of knowing God and his Word beyond just rational analysis. It is meditative and prayerful.

I also value the prayers of others. In recent years I learned of a prayer written and used daily by John Stott, the world-renowned pastor, author and leader. I have adopted this prayer as part of my daily practice. It is a wonderfully trinitarian prayer that has been immensely helpful in framing my heart and mind every morning. It is in two parts as follows.

Good morning, Heavenly Father.
Good morning, Lord Jesus.
Good morning, Holy Spirit.
Heavenly Father, I worship you as the Creator and
    Sustainer of the universe.

Lord Jesus, I worship you, Savior and Lord of the world.
Holy Spirit, I worship you, Sanctifier of the people of God.
Glory to the Father, and to the Son and to the Holy Spirit.
As it was in the beginning, is now and will be forever.
    Amen.

Heavenly Father, I pray that I may live this day in your
    presence and please you more and more.
Lord Jesus, I pray that this day I will take up my cross and
    follow you.
Holy Spirit, I pray that this day you will fill me with
    yourself
    and cause your fruit to ripen in my life:
Love, joy, peace, patience, kindness, goodness, faithfulness,
    gentleness and self-control.
Holy, blessed, and glorious Trinity, three persons in one
    God, have mercy upon me. Amen.

I use the first part of the prayer to begin my time, and then conclude my time with the second part. In between I read and reflect on the selected Bible passage from the Scripture Union notes, pray for my family and church, and then pray for my work in light of the passage I just read. I try to hear one phrase, teaching or prompting that I can pray for others and for myself that day.

However, I don't see this as just a pietistic practice or duty to make us feel or act more holy. Nor does the length or even the consistency of our devotional life directly correlate with godly living. There are all too many exceptions and serious moral failures of those who wouldn't dare skip their devotional time. But the alternative of not intentionally connecting with God is not particularly helpful either.

In the beautiful movie *The Painted Veil*, there is the compelling story of a doctor working in the interior of China trying to stem an outbreak of cholera. In that story the doctor talks with a Catholic missionary in a remote village. The missionary is a mother superior who reflects on her life moving from a love relationship with God when she became a nun in her teenage years to a relationship of duty in her older years. This dedicated woman identifies with the metaphor of a married couple that would never agree to divorce but no longer have anything to talk about. She then profoundly says, "but when love and duty are one, then grace is within you." Keeping a devotional time may seem simplistic or even perfunctory, but approaching a devotional time with both love and duty can unleash God's grace within us.

Walking with Jesus. Another dimension of dancing is walking. We learn to dance by walking through the steps of the dance while listening to a teacher or someone who already knows the dance. Again we are dependent on outside instruction. A fascinating historical example of this is the story of the two disciples who were walking to the town of Emmaus after Jesus was killed. The Gospel of Luke records that the resurrected Jesus joins them for this journey but although they talked with him about him, they did not recognize him.

However, they liked his company so much they talked him into having a meal with them. When Jesus blessed the bread and shared it with them they then knew it was Jesus who then quickly disappeared. As they discussed these very strange events they said to each other "Were not our hearts burning within us while he was talking to us on the road, while he was opening the scriptures to us?" (Lk 24:32).

Although their physical eyes did not recognize Jesus, their hearts did. There was something about Jesus' teaching of the Scriptures that created a fire of inner attraction to God. There is great value in hearing Jesus interpreting his Word to us over an extended period of time. The Ten Commandments are foundational. If we as leaders would just obey these simple instructions of not lying, not stealing, not coveting, not committing adultery, keeping the sabbath and so on, most of our ethical problems would not even occur. When we add Jesus' teaching from the Sermon on the Mount and his emphasis on the Great Commandments of loving God and neighbor, we have a comprehensive framework for the highest standards of ethical behavior and leadership practice.

But in addition to being reminded of biblical teachings there is a need for wisdom on how to apply these teachings within the specifics of our lives and jobs. Here is where we can receive spiritual discernment and a dynamic dependence on the Holy Spirit to guide us. If we want dancing hearts like those of the early disciples on the way to Emmaus, we must be able to take the time to listen to the Word of the Lord as we walk along with Jesus.

A number of years ago there was a popular book called *Are You Running with Me, Jesus?* It expressed an honest longing to know that Jesus was indeed alongside the author in the midst of a highly active life. A more recent and common expression is "Will God show up?"

I suspect we all have some variation of this question ourselves because we know we can't satisfactorily live or lead without some sense of God's presence. But because God does walk beside us even when we don't see him, perhaps a better question is "What are you saying to me, Jesus?" Because Jesus is always with us, the question is not really "Will God show up?" but "Do we recognize him?"

It is interesting to note that in the continuation of the story in Luke, the disciples met to discuss all that was happening to them after Jesus' death. Jesus again appeared to them and "opened their minds to understand the Scriptures" (Lk 24:45). This narrative illustrates that both the heart and mind are necessary to fully understand God's teachings. Sometimes we learn through the mind first, but sometimes it is our hearts that open our understanding.

PRACTICING INVOLVEMENT WITH OTHERS

We need to know about God, but we also must respond to God

and others. A dancing heart is a passionate and compassionate heart, a heart that wants to tell others that Jesus is alive, a heart that eagerly seeks fellowship with other believers, a heart that cares about the poor and issues of justice, a heart that gives us focus and context for life. A dancing heart is a heart that reflects our deepest affections.

There are many ways that we can choose to be involved with others that are not only an expression of faithfulness but also strengthen our leadership. Before I became publisher with Inter-Varsity Press, I was working with the Press's leadership team in a temporary fashion. As part of this responsibility I was with them and many other IVP employees at Urbana, the triennial mega-student missions convention sponsored by InterVarsity. IVP was there to provide a bookstore of nearly one hundred thousand books to serve the twenty thousand students in attendance.

Such a massive undertaking needed lots of people power just to unload and stack the books. Without thinking too much about it, I joined in on this work. Several months later when I officially took over as publisher I was surprised to read an internal commentary on my appointment that nicely noted my executive background but especially noted my work in the bookstore at Urbana. Since then I have always chosen to be involved with our annual inventory and other opportunities for work involvement that I don't have to do. There is always the temptation to do this just to be seen doing it, but when I freely pitch in and help others with their jobs, there is a partnership of involvement that is very satisfying and builds community.

Another experience that has helped shape my leadership ellipse occurred during the last week of my Regent College class "Quiet Heart, Dancing Heart" (see the introduction). We had convened early one morning on a beach not far from the school. The day was cool and cloudy, and no one else was around. This was a good thing because we were given a group assignment that would have made me feel very self-conscious if there had been an audience of tourists.

The assignment for our group of twenty-eight adults was to construct a large sand sculpture. This was a challenge in itself, but the particular difficulty to this assignment was that we had to do it in silence. It was quite daunting for a large group to do a sophisticated sand sculpture without talking to each other.

What we learned, though, and indeed this was the intent of the assignment, was that our words can be used to control or dominate others. This was especially true for those who liked to talk, but it was even true for those who were temperamentally quiet. We all felt somewhat powerless without the normal props of conversational banter.

We had to pay attention to each other. We had to look at each other's eyes to detect recognition or misunderstanding; we had to touch or show each other what we were doing or wanted to do; and we had to respond to the initiatives of those who just wanted to take action. It felt unnatural. I knew how to do it in theory, but just couldn't do it in practice.

Yet, we began to make progress. Someone drew a small-scale sketch of an idea that we basically agreed to work on in different small groups. Actually digging and working with the sand was very satisfying after standing around trying to get each other's attention.

However, I noticed that one in our group was not participating. She was standing with her arms crossed and communicating nonverbally (which of course was her only option at the time) that she was not particularly thrilled with this assignment. She was a fine artist in both the professional and the aesthetic sense, and I suspected that making sand castles was a bit beneath her dignity and artistic calling.

But then I noticed that she slipped away from the group and went into the nearby woods that lined the beach. She came out of the woods dragging a good-sized log. I wasn't sure what she wanted with the log but I silently offered to help her, and together we brought the log to the sand sculpture. She positioned it at the bottom of the sand sculpture.

Then she went back into the woods and brought out another log that was a bit smaller and placed it across the first log in a way that formed a cross. I was initially surprised she had done this; the cross felt too stereotypical for what was supposed to be a creative expression.

But she wasn't finished. She continued to make numerous trips across the surrounding beach picking up discarded items like a sandal with a broken strap, an empty suntan lotion bottle, used lunch bags and even some seaweed. She was picking up trash from the beach and bringing it all to the foot of the cross she had shaped with the logs.

As she was doing this, the rest of us stopped what we were doing and just watched her carry out her part of the sand sculpture. With only the sound of the water in the background we watched as she then knelt in the midst of her trash at the bottom of the cross.

By this time, we noticed that she was crying and soon we were crying too. Her dramatic enactment of bringing her junk to the cross touched all of us deeply. She was letting go of her disdain for the assignment and embracing the freedom of offering her haughty attitude to God. It was one of the most meaningful times of worship I have ever experienced—and all in quiet.

For the final several days of class after that time on the beach, that woman had a new demeanor and countenance. She was more energized and happier. Her affections for God had broken through, and she exhibited a dancing heart that stimulated her interest and involvement with the rest of us. She had experienced a touch of spiritual transformation that was changing her relationships. She was living with a connectedness in her spiritual life.

Pursuing this kind of integrity is a long-term and comprehensive endeavor. It necessarily involves spiritual contentment in

God, a rejection of that which hinders our growth, a renewed way of thinking and a buoyancy of spirit that energizes us for involvement with others. When we have a dancing heart of inner integrity, we are better able to pursue integrity and involvement in our outer world.

Yet we cannot dance all of the time. Leadership is difficult, and there are many burdens and demands that weigh heavily on us. Even Jesus was prophesied to be a "man of sorrows and acquainted with grief." A dancing heart is not a sanguine heart or a heart with a peppy perspective that always sees the glass as half full.

Rather a dancing heart is alive with the Word and Spirit of God and being in the presence of God that responds to the people and needs in our world. My prayer in my rule of life is that I want to have "a dancing heart that is attentive to others and engages the world around me with God and his Kingdom." As leaders we may have different styles of dancing, but we cannot afford a life of mere marching that does not get involved with others.

PART TWO

SHAPING OUR
OUTER WORLD

FIVE

IN A FRENZIED WORLD

The Perspective of Prayer

*A gazelle wakes up every morning knowing that it will have to
run faster than the fastest lion in order to stay alive.
A lion wakes up knowing that it will have to run
faster than the slowest gazelle in order to stay alive.
Whether you are a gazelle or a lion, you wake up every morning
knowing that you will have to run faster to stay alive.*

AFRICAN PROVERB

A cartoon in *The New Yorker* shows two couples in a grocery
market. As they hurriedly head in opposite directions, one couple
says over their shoulders to the other couple "You're on our 'to do'
list." The broad smiles on all four figures communicate nonchalance
at the irony of seemingly wanting to get together but not
having time to do so or even talk about it.

As leaders we are often in the same position. We genuinely want
to slow down and be with people, but our pace of life does not allow
it. "You're so busy" or "I'm really busy right now" are statements
that describe our realities, but they also have become a
badge of honor. We take pride in our busyness even when we feel
smothered by it.

THE REASONS FOR HURRY SICKNESS

Why is this? Why are we so "captured" by our busyness? Why is it so energizing and addictive at the same time? Why are so many books written about our frenetic lifestyles? Why do we diagnose people for "hurry sickness" or flippantly talk about our "hurry-go-round"? Why can't we slow down without jeopardizing our jobs or ignoring our responsibilities?

Let me suggest that there are two fundamental sets of reasons for our overstretched lives. These reasons are like two tributaries rushing into in a muddy organizational river that floods our ability to cope effectively with all of the demands we face in leadership. Understanding the power of their combined current helps us to see our need for divine wisdom and strength in order to better navigate this rushing river of contemporary life.

External complexities. The first set of reasons come from outside pressures. "Sleep is a crutch," says Zach Thomas, the founder of *Ranger Coffee*, which is one of many hyper-caffeinated blends of coffee. Although the coffee may be new, the predisposition to be in a hurry is a long-standing pattern of American life. The noted French sociologist Alexis de Tocqueville wrote in 1840 about "the feverish ardor" with which Americans pursue material gains and private pleasures. Now the whole industrialized world has imbibed this pace of life for similar allurements.

In a more recent commentary on reading, Robert Samuelson writes about the "sad fate of the comma" and its increasing disuse in all forms of written and electronic communication. He suggests that this reduction of punctuation is a metaphor for our frantic culture. "The comma is, after all, a small sign that flashes PAUSE. It tells the reader to slow down a bit, and then move on."

Our culture increasingly rejects this kind of punctuation in both our organizational and spiritual lives.

We are immersed if not enmeshed in an exploding, digitized, fast company culture that is exhausting. Alvin Toffler predicted this in his prophetic 1970s book *Future Shock*, where he used culture shock as a metaphor for the disorienting experience we have in trying to live in the foreign culture of things moving too fast. Our previously successful patterns for making decisions, supervising people, casting vision and managing our daily schedule seem to be ineffective and swamped with new ways and opportunities to do things. We may feel inferior to teenagers' computer skills and multitasking abilities, and we exhibit what is sometimes referred to as multiple-choice syndrome. We are shocked by how much we have to do.

Another external complexity is the increasing demands on organizational life—whether in a huge corporation or a local church. When Henry Ford mass-produced his Model T, he decided that they could be any color as long as it was black. He also said that the only things he wanted from his workers were their hands. Such autocratic but simple decision making is no longer tolerated or even possible in an open-ended environment of choice and participation. People want ownership and involvement.

Yet at the same time there are the massive governmental and insurance regulations that are so invasive. As a result of the Enron scandal, the Sorbaynes-Oxley Act has extensive compliance requirements for financial standards and reporting. The same can be said for the security demands of the Patriot Act in the wake of 9/11. These increasing external controls combined with increasing internal organizational demands for more freedom create tremendous tension and weariness for leaders. We find that it takes far longer to do our jobs with adequate time for good group processes while simultaneously complying with uncompromising legal demands.

One of my favorite quotes from Oliver Wendell Holmes is when he said he "wouldn't give a fig for simplicity this side of complexity but he would give his life for simplicity on the other side of complexity." Even though he wrote this long before our current explosion of complexity, Holmes realized that we cannot live a stable and satisfying life mired in complexity. The fatigue is too debilitating.

But he also realized that avoiding complexity yields a simplicity that is not true to life. None of us want simplistic answers to genuine problems. What Holmes longed for instead was the wisdom of simplicity that does not deny our external complexities but understands them and responds to them simply and successfully.

However, our external complexities make up only one of the tributaries that threaten to drown us in our frenzied world. The other and less publicized tributary is made up of our self-inflicted internal compulsions.

Internal compulsions. Perhaps the more dangerous threat to spiritual and organizational life is what I call "the tower of Babel complex." Just as those ancients in Genesis 11 wanted to build a tower that would reach to the sky in order to make a name for themselves, there seems to be a compulsive drive in all organizations to build a name for ourself as well. Stockholders demand it, boards of trustees expect it, mission agencies cannot raise money effectively without it, and pastors feel pressured to produce it. Despite the unquestioned biblical value of humility, there is a driving source of pride within us that wants us to raise our index finger in the air and shout "we're number one." The kingdom of God can sometimes look more like a football game of strategies, cheerleading and posturing than the presence and rule of Jesus.

When this occurs, our tower of Babel falls into confusion and fragmentation. We become top-heavy with our ego and self-centered vision. This happens to some extent in all organizations, including those with the highest conscious motivation of serving God. In fact sometimes our inflated sense of importance in doing the work of God hinders us from seeing what is happening within our own structure and our soul.

Although it is not a surprise to learn of scandals in politics and the business world that are fueled by the lure of greater money and power, there are far too many churches, faith-based colleges and Christian organizations that pursue financial growth and expansion of their mission to such an extent that they lose touch with what it means to follow the teachings of Scripture with respect to relational integrity. Making a name for ourself eclipses declaring the glory of God. We become exhausted in our self-promotion. We become consumed with the compulsions of building our personal and organizational towers.

I struggle continually with this tension, which is another expression of the leadership ellipse. One focal point wants to humbly love God while the other wants to command public recognition of Inter-Varsity Press being a leading publisher of thoughtful Christian books. Is it possible to be aggressively proud of our churches, organizations and ministries but to personally remain humble?

I believe the answer can be yes, but not in an automatic way that answers the question once and for all, because once we think we have achieved humility we have lost it. Who we are and how we lead are constantly being shaped by our dialogue with God about this basic human compulsion of pride. However, even though our compulsions are often displayed publicly, the roots of compulsions are internal. Listen to the compulsions in the following poem.

> If an expert does not have some problem to vex him, he is
>   unhappy!
> If a philosopher's teaching is never attacked, she pines
>   away!
> He who wants followers seeks political power.
> She who wants reputation, holds an office.
> The strong man looks for weights to lift.
> The brave woman looks for an emergency in which she can
>   show bravery.

Where would the gardener be if there were no more weeds?
What would become of business without a market of fools?
Produce! Get results! Make money! Make Friends! Make
    changes!
Or you will die of despair!

This poem, called "Active Life," sounds like it was written yesterday in the way it describes a compulsive drive toward achievements and recognition. Yet it was actually written in the fourth-century B.C.! I interpret from this that we can't just blame our busyness on our culture, our upbringing, our church or our organization. There is something deep within each of us that makes us want to be the Creator rather than the created. It is this sinful proclivity that is the real root of our compulsions.

Consequently the solution to our problems is not just better time management or greater managerial competence. Organizational leadership and management require very hard professional work, and we need all the help we can get. But although professional expertise may be necessary at times, it is never sufficient to help us with our deepest needs.

What complicates things for Christian leaders are the compulsions related to Christian ministry, like commitment and intentionality. This is a difficult and delicate area to talk about because we are called to "take up our cross" and live lives of obedience to the Lord. But we also need to be very aware of how strong dedication and intentionality can become self-absorbed and destructive. I suspect we all know people whose sense of personal vision becomes off-putting to us, and they hinder the work of God as they trample over those who stand in their way. What we may not know is how we also do that to others.

A PRAYER TO GUIDE US

So how do we wade through these rushing currents of external complexities and internal compulsions? I faced this question in a gut-checking way when I was asked to present several Bible teachings to about sixty Christian leaders. The assignment was to speak to the issues of not having enough emotional, physical and spiritual "capacity" to cope with the opportunities and challenges of their leadership.

I was reluctant to do this for several reasons. First, I had my own capacity problems. In addition to my normal workload and travel obligations, I was leading a retreat of our leadership team the following week and needed to prepare for two board meetings plus teach an adult elective in our church. I felt overworked and didn't know how I could get a better handle on my own life, let alone have the time to prepare something meaningful to help others. At least I could identify with the problem. But by accepting this assignment would I be helping to solve the problem or just publicly illustrating it?

The bigger concern for me though was, did I have a word from the Lord for not only these leaders but myself as well? My first flippant thought was that I couldn't wait to hear what I had to say! But in a more serious vein, I wanted to have a frame of reference that would speak with biblical authority to this group. I knew that this assignment required more than just my own ideas and experience, and also more than just better principles of time management. These were senior leaders who had read all of the management books and were still struggling.

As I pondered this request, I was praying the Lord's Prayer. Although I had prayed this prayer thousands of times, it was at that moment that I had a clear sense that this familiar prayer of Jesus provided a discerning pathway for me to live in my frenzied world.

This familiar teaching of Jesus is recorded in two places and in two different contexts. The first time is in the middle of the Sermon on the Mount in Matthew 6. The other passage is in Luke 11 and comes immediately after the story of Jesus' dialogue with Martha when she was upset with all the work she had to do while Mary was just listening to Jesus. I believe this linking of events in Luke is not accidental but connects what Jesus taught about prayer in the context of Martha's busyness.

Using the more familiar teaching in Matthew, though, the prayer begins with addressing our heavenly Father and then identifies six requests in two groups of three. The first three relate to God—his name, his kingdom and his will on earth. The second three focus on our needs—our daily bread, our giving and receiving forgiveness, and our need for protection and deliverance. Let me share some of my reflections on this prayer that have shaped not only what I said in my talks but what I have subsequently tried to practice.

Our. The little plural pronoun *our* teaches the importance of the communal dimension of this prayer, which is linked to a relationship with God the Father. It is a main reason this prayer has been prayed together throughout the history of the church. We are all children of God. This is the basis of our unity and is an invitation to bring our family stuff to the Father.

So we can pray for and with each other in this battle against our busyness. One way is to collectively acknowledge the problem and streamline our expectations for each other. Some companies intentionally don't have meetings on Monday mornings, and some churches set aside evenings as family nights with no church activities allowed. Avoiding electronic communication and work on the sabbath also gives us some spiritual breathing room. These are not dramatic or unique decisions, but making them together is far more effective than having to work out everything alone.

Father. Unfortunately, due to a world filled with abusive male relationships, the term *father* (or *Daddy* in the Aramaic language of Jesus) for God instills feelings of repulsion rather than intimacy. So many children have grown up with such a distant or even a nonexistent father that God too seems far away, unapproachable or someone to be feared.

Yet I think this is why the term and its implied relationship with God are so important. We need and crave a loving intimacy with God our Father that is neither rushed nor based on fear.

I have great memories from my childhood of jumping into bed with my dad on Saturday mornings and wrestling with him. What was so much fun is that he seemed to enjoy this playfulness as much as I did. Then as a father, I have had the reciprocal joy of the same kind of joyful wrestling matches with our daughters. There is a freedom in that type of relationship that is deeply immediate and uncalculated.

The most vivid image, though, that comes to my mind is that of our granddaughter Eden, who was born with Down syndrome. When she was two years old, she and her mother were visiting us while her father, Eric, was away. Although Eden was not talking, it was great for us to see her scooting around on the floor and jabbering her responses to life. One evening, Alice had the idea of taking a picture of Eric from our refrigerator and showing it to Eden. She paused just a second and then reached out with her arms to the picture and said "Daddy!" Even though Eric wasn't in the room physically, there was a spontaneous joy of recognition and love in Eden for her father.

This exemplified the kind of loving relationship that does not promote or succumb to frenzy, because it delights in the moment. It is a relationship that increases our faith that God is with us even if we can't literally see him. Practically, I find it helpful at times to pray to "Daddy" and enjoy the specialness of that simple term of endearment.

In heaven. This seems like a strange descriptor after such a term of affection for our Father. What does it mean for "Daddy" to be in heaven, or so far removed from us? Augustine countered the ancient notion that "in heaven" is a spatial description when he wrote "God is not closer to the birds or to tall people"! Rather, "in heaven" is an attribution of God's character. Our Father is not limited to our experience or imagination. God is distinct and separate from us. God is beyond us. In theological terms he transcends creation.

I have gained a better understanding of how God can be immanent (or close) and transcendent at the same time through St. Bonaventure, who lived in the thirteenth century. He was not only a follower and biographer of Francis of Assisi but was also the dean of the University of Paris. He was a wonderful combination of a deeply spiritual intellectual.

Bonaventure wrote of a vision he had of a six-winged seraph with the two bottom wings overlapping the seraph's feet. He suggested that one of the two bottom wings is the wing of creation and that in our spiritual journey we must see that we are part of God's eternal plan in the universe. We are created in God's image for eternity.

But the second bottom wing is the wing of the body, which reminds us of our limitations. We are not God and have to live within the limits of who we have been created to be. It is when the two wings cross that we experience wholeness and freedom in our relationship to God. Knowing that God is in heaven releases us from having to do everything ourselves and enables us to trust God even more. Our belief in God in heaven does not mitigate against an intimacy with God but rather magnifies it. Or as the old children's prayer said it so well, "God is great and God is good."

When I feel most frenzied is usually when I am least in touch with God and tempted to pursue my own greatness. When I rest in the God who is "in heaven," my world is put into a more proper perspective.

Hallowed be your name. The first request in Jesus' prayer is to hallow the name of God. This may be the most overlooked of all the requests because it is easy to be thrown off by the word *hal-*

lowed. It sounds traditional and archaic, like when we refer to the hallowed halls of ivy.

But *hallowed* is another word for holy, which is neither a democratic nor egalitarian word but ascribes a special association to the name of God. It is consistent with the third of the Ten Commandments, which warns against taking the name of God in vain. We primarily apply this to not cursing, but it also refers to not using the name of God for our own purposes. Leaders can easily engage in a form of divine name-dropping, like when we suggest that "the Lord told me" as a way to add to our authority.

In the last book of the Old Testament, the prophet Malachi repeatedly encourages the people to honor the name of the Lord. He even makes the stark contrast between those who do evil and those who revere the name of the Lord. And the poetic promise for such reverence was that "for you who revere my name the sun of righteousness shall rise, with healing in its wings. You shall go out leaping like calves from the stall" (Mal 4:2). I suspect that we all need healing from the effects of our compulsions, and that we all desire to have the boundless energy of a young calf rather than the burdens of busyness. Thus we pray for God's name to be revered and hallowed in our speech and in our lives.

Your kingdom come, your will be done. These two requests go together because the second is really an extension of the first. One of the current leadership principles being promoted in many books is that of organizational alignment. Like a car that needs its tires aligned for a smoother ride, organizations need to have all of their parts aligned in the same direction.

In a parallel way the Lord asks us to pray for our spiritual alignment so that we are in sync with God's kingdom and his will. Our lives as Christians are not just eschatological or for the future, but are to be a part of God's work on earth. These are requests for the rule of God now—in the church and in the world. But what might this mean with respect to our capacity problems? Let me suggest the practice of corporate spiritual discernment.

In Scripture there are at least three types of discernment of God's intentions. The first is the leader model. Here God speaks to an individual like Moses, and the people are to follow. There are times when leaders need that direct sense of God's presence and direction. But as Moses discovered when he angrily struck the rock out of his own leadership frustrations, we leaders should not presume that God is always speaking through us. Leadership is often lonely, but it should never be presumptuous.

The second form of discernment is actually the most common in Scripture and is a form of voting through the casting of lots. This seems a bit primitive in contrast to Roberts Rules of Order or other sophisticated means of group process. But it can express a certain faith in God's circumstantial direction in our corporate decision making. We try to do what is right with what we do know and subsequently and prayerfully "roll the dice" in making decisions about an unknown and uncertain future.

The third is the process of thoughtful spiritual community. A good example of this is in the first-century Jerusalem council recorded in Acts 15. Some of the Jewish Christian leaders were aghast that Gentiles had become believers. They wanted these converts to be circumcised to declare their new identity. Understandably, the Gentiles didn't want to be circumcised and questioned whether this was a necessary part of the gospel. There was quite a conflict until James, who was leading the council, made a reasonable compromise decision. The Gentiles did not have to be circumcised, but they did have to conform to some other behavior patterns.

What is so interesting about this story is James's observation that "it has seemed good to the Holy Spirit and to us" to make this decision. I believe that this is a marvelous example of godly reason being used. It represents neither a stark rationality nor an uninformed spirituality.

This is a mark of God's kingdom and God's will. There is a holy collaboration of human processes and divine blessing. Such partnership often takes extra time for prayer and for careful conversation. Times of extended silence are also opportunities for a group to better hear each other and the promptings of the Holy Spirit. When we pray for God's kingdom, it takes the focus away from our kingdom and compulsions. It also helps us withstand the currents of our compulsions.

Give us this day our daily bread. These last three requests cover the spectrum of time in our life experiences—the present, the past and the future. The request for daily bread is for sustenance for the present. There are many ideas of what Jesus actually meant by this as the specific word for "daily" was not used anywhere else in ancient literature. In fact the early church father Origin thought Matthew made it up!

Many have interpreted this as a basis for daily Mass or the Eucharist. Others see it in a spiritual way because Jesus referred to himself as the "bread of life." Yet others, and especially those in the poorer parts of the world, interpret it quite literally as daily physical food.

All of these may be true in some sense, but I want to suggest the Old Testament metaphor of manna as being particularly significant for us. Manna was good only for a day at a time. The Israelites could not hoard manna. There was a strong present tense to manna that meant they did not have to be anxious for the next day. It would always be there (see Ex 16:13-20).

In praying for our daily bread I wonder if we might also consider the spiritual discipline of fasting. Although in the Old Testament fasting is primarily a sign of repentance, it is also a practice that reminds us of our dependence on God. Perhaps we might consider fasting as a practice for not only limiting food at times but also other parts of life that have become gluttonous—like information, instant availability or even meetings!

We live in a market-driven culture of needing more because it is possible. But fasting means we don't have to fulfill every desire or idea. It is a voluntary denial of something good for something better. The request is for our daily needs, not for unlimited possibilities.

So it is important to recognize what our true needs are and share them honestly with God. A wonderful example of this comes from Pope John XXIII, when he was presiding over the weighty Vatican II Council. Evidently, every night at the end of a long day of discussions he would go into the chapel and pray, "Jesus, this is your church. I'm going to bed."

And forgive us our debts, as we also have forgiven our debtors. This teaching directs us to the past and the relationships that burden our souls. It is probably the clearest cause-and-effect teaching in all of Scripture. It is not only mentioned twice but is the only part of the prayer that is subsequently explained in careful detail. The clear teaching is that if we don't forgive others, neither will our Father forgive us.

However, this seems so arbitrary and almost a divine tit-for-tat arrangement. But to paraphrase Martin Luther, how can we have open hands to receive God's forgiveness when they are clenched in anger and vindictiveness toward others? Forgiveness draws us to the very character of God, and as Augustine said, we are "more like God in the act of forgiveness than any other moment." But why don't we more readily forgive others? It is not only commanded but seems so right to do. From my own experience and observations, I think there are several reasons.

The first is we don't like to forgive others because they no longer will be in our debt. We are releasing power over them. We can no longer think, *You owe me.* But, to quote Lewis Smedes, "when you forgive someone you release a person from bondage, and that person is yourself." An unforgiving heart is a hard heart, and we will not be spiritually effective leaders with such a resistance to grace and forgiveness.

A second reason is that we feel it would be hypocritical or exhibit a lack of integrity to forgive someone we really can't forgive at the time. We don't want to pretend. This is honorable to a point, but it doesn't provide forgiveness and can even promote a self-righteousness about our own honesty.

A third reason is that we may be afraid of what would be perceived as cheap grace, and that the person we are forgiving will do it again to us. So we won't forgive until the person earns our trust or proves that he or she is repentant.

I struggle with these last two reasons because they seem so plausible and understandable. However, they do not fit with the teaching that Jesus gave us. When we withhold forgiveness from others (for whatever reason) we are putting ourselves in the role of God or even being superior to God, who freely extends his grace and forgiveness to us time and time again.

Jesus taught us to forgive people seventy times seven if necessary, and this gives us insight as to how hard forgiveness is. We usually can't just forgive someone or ourselves once and be done with it. The pain of sin is too deep, and we need to keep forgiving others as often as they sin against us and maybe even for the same sin. But by doing so, we live into forgiveness more and understand more of God's forgiveness to us.

The freedom to forgive is not easy, nor should it be. Forgiving someone too quickly may well be an avoidance of working out the relationship in a deeper way. It also may mean that we haven't really forgiven the person but want to appear as though we have!

But neither should forgiveness be postponed until the other person truly repents and asks for forgiveness. Nor should we wait until we feel like forgiving someone. Often when there is deep hurt, as in ethnic conflicts or long-term family dysfunctions, there may never be confession or the feeling of wanting to forgive those who have hurt us.

Yet, the Lord says that his forgiveness is directly related to our willingness to forgive others. This means that we do not receive God's forgiveness when we have not forgiven others in our family, office or at church. I have experienced this to be true. When I hold on to resentments or conflicts with others, I am not able to work with them with a glad heart. But when I forgive them, I am free to encourage and enjoy them.

So we forgive and we pray for forgiveness. N. T. Wright says forgiveness of one another and receiving God's forgiveness is a "central part of our deliverance from evil." I am discovering that forgiving others helps release me from the evil addiction to a frenzied life.

And do not bring us to the time of trial, but rescue us from the evil one. This request is for the future and has created much discussion about what it means since God does not tempt anyone. It is true that God tests us but does not allow us to be tempted beyond what we can endure. So we pray for his protection from temptation and deliverance when we are tempted. Sometimes I need this discipline when I begin to think or talk negatively about someone. I pray "lead me not into temptation" and this exercise helps me to not go there.

The example of Jesus being tempted in the wilderness is of great value in understanding this. Not only is there evil in the world that we try to avoid, but there is also an evil one who seeks to draw us away from God. We cannot resist the evil one just through self-discipline. We need the power of God's deliverance.

DISCIPLINES OF RESTRAINT

All of these disciplines of discernment, of fasting, forgiveness and deliverance, are actually disciplines of restraint—not of doing more but of not doing as much. In fact, I believe the word of the Lord to us in our challenge of busyness and work overload is both "don't do so much" and "Lord, teach us to pray."

The challenge for us as leaders is not just to fix our internal world by trying to eliminate the sin that bubbles up within us through dedicated self-discipline. Dallas Willard calls this approach "sin-management." It yields some benefit at first but ultimately is spiritually ineffective because it puts our "self" in control, which is at the heart of our sinful nature. Sheer effort, no matter how well intentioned, does not lead to a life of grace.

Nor is it sufficient to just do a better job of managing our time and utilizing our leadership power to better control our outer world. Again, such practices are valuable to a point but do not help us deal with the necessary messiness of leadership. If we really could completely control our outside world to be free from unsolvable problems, we would not be needed as leaders.

Furthermore, our internal compulsions and external complexities act synergistically against us. These dynamics of personal struggle make spiritual leadership in a broken world extremely difficult and impossible to solve by our own effort. This is why the Lord invites us to pray. We need the instruction and infusion of God's Spirit to convict and guide us in our decisions. Prayer then becomes not just a discipline to practice but a pathway for our lives.

I know a woman who works with Alzheimer's patients—people unable to verbally communicate what they are thinking or to even know what they are thinking. She struggled to know how such patients pray and came to the conclusion that prayer for them is their lives rather than their words. She then realized that this is also true for everyone. Our lives reflect our communion with God and our prayers teach us to live such lives.

Most Christians throughout the world pray the Lord's Prayer weekly, and many do so on a daily basis. Although that was not my tradition, it has become my practice. As I pray this prayer either privately or in community it is both a reminder and a request for God's grace.

The Lord taught us to pray—to pray for discernment, to pray

for his kingdom, to pray for our daily needs, to pray with others and to pray for forgiveness. It is a prayer of relationship and of obedience. Such prayer gives us perspective and purpose in living in our frenzied world.

SIX

IN A LONELY WORLD

The Promise of Belonging

Because we love something else more than this world,
we love even this world better than those who know no other.

C. S. LEWIS

My God, my God, why have you forsaken me?" is the most startling and anguished cry of loneliness and desolation in the history of the world. Jesus, the Son of God, who only days before said, "I and my Father are one," felt completely alone and rejected not only by those he came to save but also by God the Father. It makes the cliché "It is lonely at the top" extraordinarily trivial in comparison. No matter how misunderstood or isolated we may feel as leaders, we cannot comprehend the complete sense of isolation that Jesus experienced on the cross.

But part of the glory of the gospel is that because of his sufferings, Jesus understands our loneliness in a far deeper way than we can imagine. Despite our despair that no one else either knows or understands what we might be going through, Jesus does. The great spiritual says it well: "Nobody knows the trouble I've seen. Nobody knows but Jesus." Whether or not we suffer physically, we often suffer emotionally and spiritually in our leadership responsibilities. We can be lonely despite and even because of all the people around us. We may call it positional distance or blame others for it, but loneliness is often a part of our leadership. It is also something we can bring upon ourselves.

LONELINESS OF OVERWORK

America has been called "the republic of overwork." As leaders we imbibe this cultural influence. We are tempted to believe that the more we work, the better things will be, and to some degree that is true. When we put in those extra hours early in the morning or late at night or during weekends and holidays, we are able to accomplish more and add value and direction to our organizations and those we lead. Conversely if we are lazy or contain our leadership so that we don't work more than our designated forty hours, we lose some of our leadership edge with ourselves and with others.

However, our busyness not only reflects our frenzied culture, it is also in a counterintuitive way the seedbed for leadership loneliness. Because our work as leaders is never done and because work can be addictive, it is easy to lose boundaries. We then believe that we have to be in the office those extra hours just to be competitive or that we have to get on the plane again to be at that conference or to solve those intractable personnel problems in another city. We morph from being effective in leading others to being exhausted in being led by the demands of others.

Jesus knew these pressures as well. He was no slacker. Jesus got up early to pray, and visited his disciples at night while they were fishing. But he also said, "Come to me, all you that are weary and are carrying heavy burdens, and I will give you rest" (Mt 11:28). Jesus took time away to rest and to pray. As Jesus' close disciple, Peter tells us not to exhaust ourselves with worry but to "cast all your anxiety on [Jesus], because he cares for you" (1 Pet 5:7). It is interesting and instructive that in the verse immediately preceding this exhortation, Peter tells us to humble ourselves, or as Eugene Peterson translates it "be content with who you are." Overwork is frequently a sign of discontent. We are trying to do something or be somebody that is beyond who we were created to be. We are looking for satisfaction in the wrong place.

David Benner tells the story from Middle Eastern folklore of a fellow named Nasrudin who when going home one night realized he had lost his key. He tried searching for it but it was too dark to see. So he went out by the streetlight to look there. A neighbor noticed him on his hands and knees and joined him in looking for the lost key. After some time of futile searching the neighbor asked him if he was sure he had lost the key where they were looking. Nasrudin replied, "No, I didn't lose it here. I lost it in my house." His bewildered neighbor responded, "Then why are you looking for it out here?" "Because," Nasrudin said, "the light is so much better here." Sometimes because we are only looking for satisfaction in our work, we forget where we actually lost our key to contentment.

I realized this several years ago while on a vacation in Alaska. I was trying to unwind from the intensity of how I had been living life. I was standing at the railing of the ship taking pictures of glaciers and realizing I was running out of memory on my digital camera. I started deleting some previous pictures so that I could add more.

It then occurred to me that my life had been like a digital camera memory card that only could absorb more as I sadly let go of something else that had been important. I had no extra capacity. Overwork leads to similar feelings. We can't enjoy the past or even the present because of how we are trying to keep adding more to our lives. Such a lack of enjoyment quickly leads to discontent and loneliness in our leadership.

LONELINESS OF BOREDOM

Henri Nouwen once made the observation that so many people are bored and busy at the same time. I think this is particularly true with leaders. There is no end to how busy we are, but we may not consciously identify our boredom and its synergistic relationship with busyness. Nor may we realize that boredom is a great precursor and reason for deep feelings of loneliness.

Guilt is the burden of the past, and anxiety is the burden of the future. But boredom is the weighty malaise of the present tense when we feel insignificant or understimulated. In fact one of the reasons we may keep so busy is the fear of being bored. It is like always having to be electronically connected, always having to talk or always having to act. We are afraid of silence and of quiet. Esther de Waal says we are afraid of the "deafening noise of ourselves."

Ironically, though, our very attempts to avoid boredom eventually produce it. We become addicted to work and to our own adrenalin such that we need more and more to feel satisfied until we collapse and wind up with a hangover of boredom and loneliness, which can then lead to destructive behavior.

This was what happened to King David. He was an extremely successful king who "won a name for himself" by defeating his enemies one after another. Scripture says "the Lord gave victory to David wherever he went." But shortly after this observation, David chose to stay home and not to go to war against the Ammonites.

Left alone in the king's house, David was probably bored and lonely. And he committed adultery with Bathsheba and then murdered her husband to protect himself. When David backed away from his leadership as king, he was susceptible to loneliness and subsequently abused his power in very destructive ways for himself, his family and his kingdom.

Another form of boredom and loneliness comes through the weariness of routine or lack of excitement in our lives. The desert fathers called this *acedia*. It means boredom or a restlessness that can lead to sloth and a lack of personal disciplines. In *Water from a Deep Well*, Gerald Sittser says acedia was known as the "noonday demon" in monasteries, where monks grew tired from their routines of work and prayer. When our work is not exciting or continuously stimulating, we too can become tired of routine.

In response, some leaders become withdrawn and build a fortress mentality that doesn't let anyone inside their emotional struggles for fear of appearing weak. Others pursue sexual escapades or pornography to find solace for their inner discontent. Some grasp at external perks of money and the status it can buy, while others continually pursue other jobs. Many of us become defensive and irritable if we feel unappreciated for all of our hard work.

I once had a leader who thrived as someone who loved to "put out fires." If there was a financial problem, he would immediately call a meeting no matter what anyone else was doing at the time. He was a tremendous crisis manager who loved the thrill of making decisions under pressure. He didn't like to be alone in his job.

Unfortunately when there weren't any fires, he felt compelled to start some. He was constantly reorganizing and calling for change that created problems requiring his abilities to solve them. Some of the fires he started were good in cleaning out dead brush that builds in organizations, but others led to debilitating relational blazes. His boredom and loneliness in organizational life without a crisis eventually led to his downfall as an effective leader.

How do we get out of this bind of feeling lonely while surrounded by people? If loneliness is inevitable in leadership, how do we cope with it in ways that are not destructive? How do we cope with our own struggles in ways that are healthy for those we lead and not just as a way of meeting our own needs?

The example of Jesus' prayers is again tremendously valuable to us. After the last Passover supper with his disciples, Jesus prayed for us who would follow after him.

THE PRAYER OF JESUS

I grew up in a church that referred to Jesus' prayer in John 17 as the real Lord's Prayer. I wasn't sure of the reasons for preempting the status of the traditional Lord's Prayer, but I knew that this prayer was significant. It is not only much longer and could not be easily recited by rote, but it also reveals some deep thoughts and feelings of Jesus about belonging.

> I am no longer in the world, but they are in the world, and I am coming to you. Holy Father, protect them in your name that you have given me, so that they may be one, as we are one. . . . I am not asking you to take them out of the world, but I ask you to protect them from the evil one. They do not belong to the world, just as I do not belong to the world. Sanctify them in the truth; your word is truth. As you have sent me into the world, so I have sent them into the world. (Jn 17:11, 15-18)

Although Jesus prayed this prayer nearly two thousand years ago, I still struggle with his paradoxical request to live *in* the world without at the same time being *of* the world. How do I do this? How do all of us as Christian leaders live purposefully in our world without allowing the purposes of the world to live in us?

One place to start is realizing that we live with paradoxes all of the time. For instance, we have more time-saving devices than ever but paradoxically less time. We have inanimate computers that can talk to us even when our families can't. Physicists and mathematicians strive to discover a unified theory of the universe while their literature colleagues across campus boldly claim that there is no such metanarrative of life. Intolerance is not tolerated. We eat "jumbo shrimp" and the smallest coffee we can buy is "tall." The noted British author Charles Handy wrote a whole book on our present world titled *The Age of Paradox*.

However, I believe that the main paradox we face in our relationship with the world is not so much an intellectual or organizational as it is a moral one. E. B. White writes, "If the world were merely seductive, that would be easy. If it were merely challenging, that would be no problem. But I arise in the morning, torn between a desire to save the world and to savor the world. That makes it hard to plan the day." So how do we plan our day? How do we market our product in ways that are not manipulative? How do we teach in ways that are not condescending? What exactly are God's intentions for us as leaders in our daily jobs?

I believe that the key to understanding our Lord's prayer in John 17 is in the significance of Jesus' prayer about the importance of belonging. Jesus first affirms that we belong to the Father and to himself: "all mine are yours and yours are mine." Then Jesus prays that we will belong to each other that "we may be one." Then he declares that although we do not belong to the world, we do belong in the world. According to Jesus' prayer for us, we belong to God, we belong to each other and we belong in the world. It is in the cohesiveness and practice of these three relationships that we find direction and integrity in our outer and often lonely world.

BELONGING TO GOD

Belonging has a far deeper meaning than just a statement of formal relationship. Belonging is a strong word of identity. Whenever we walk into a room or meet with new people, we are always asking either consciously or subconsciously, *Do I belong here? Will I like being here? Will I feel like myself here?* We have a need to belong because belonging is really "a longing to be." It is a longing to be who we are created to be. It is a longing to be with those who know us and love us, and ultimately it is a longing to be with our heavenly Father.

Augustine wrote at the very beginning of his *Confessions*, "for you made us for yourself and our hearts are restless until they find their rest in you." Jesus prays for us as spiritually restless people who belong to God. This deep sense of belonging to God is essential for an effective presence in the world. When we don't have that security, we are either scared to be in the world and shyly avoid conflict over faith issues or we are arrogant in our self-importance and have very little to say that others want to hear.

Recently I was asked in an interview "Why are there so many angry atheists?" My immediate response was that it seems that they are afraid of Christians imposing their faith and morality and culture on them. They are not responding to people of faith with deep appreciation for the "aroma of Christ" in their lives. Rather they are repelled with what they detect as the odor of imposition and hypocrisy.

As surveys and interviews repeatedly show, one of the greatest hindrances to people becoming Christians is the reputation of Christians. It is also true that one of the greatest reasons for people to become Christians is the friendship and faith of other Christians they know. How do we attract people to Jesus without repelling them at the same time?

The key to being honest and even bold in our faith without being judgmental and hypocritical seems to be connected with the integrity of our relationship with God. In addition to the Father's protection, Jesus also prays for our holiness, which means our becoming more like him. In God's economy, belonging begets becoming. *Christian* literally means a "little Christ." So the more we belong to Jesus, the more we become like Jesus and the more we directly and indirectly call attention to him.

In a broadly Christian culture this may not be so noticeable, but the more secular and even pagan a culture becomes, the more belonging to God stands out. The brilliant French mathematician Blaise Pascal wrote, "When everything is moving at once, nothing appears to be moving, as on board a ship. When everyone is moving toward depravity, no one seems to be moving, but if someone stops, he shows up the others who are rushing on, by acting as a fixed point."

Being such a fixed point is integral to our calling and life in the world. We are not called to hide from the world in rigid obscurity. But neither are we called to blend in with the world such that we too are being carried along on Pascal's ship.

Not long ago a pastor confided to me that one of his great frustrations is that the church does not make more of a difference in the world. He wonders (and doubts) whether people who come to his church live any differently from those who don't go to church. Do they put their money, time and behavior where their mouths and signed doctrinal affirmations are? Although at times I share this pastor's pessimism about significant Christian influence in the world, I am also encouraged when I hear of how God has used and continues to use Christians in bringing about good.

Historically we see the profound example of William Wilberforce. Although he was a wealthy man and a member in the British Parliament from age twenty-one to sixty-five, he did not rest on his wealth or his political power. Because of his strong Christian convictions he led the battle for the abolition of the African slave trade that consumed nearly forty-six years of his life. He was finally successful three days before he died.

But in addition to this monumental accomplishment, Wilberforce also initiated sixty-five social agencies for such things as prison reform, animal shelters and establishing the first national gallery of art. At one point in his life he wondered whether he should "praise the Lord or change the world." In the movie *Amazing Grace*, Hannah Smith challenged him that by God's grace he could do both. Lest he wander from that commitment, his mentor and former slave trader John Newton wrote, "It is hoped and believed that the Lord has raised you up for the good of His church and for the good of the nation."

A contemporary example in the academic world is Ken Elzinga, an economics professor at the University of Virginia. When Ken began his teaching career there after getting his Ph.D. from Michigan State, he was warned by a colleague not to let other faculty see the Bible on his desk or he definitely would not receive tenure. At one point some of his faculty colleagues evidently had a heavy philosophical debate about whether Ken was sane or not because of his faith. Their argument was that if Ken said he talked and listened to a little green man on his shoulder, people would think he was crazy. So why wasn't he crazy when he said he talked and listened to Jesus?

But after forty years of teaching more than thirty-five thousand students at the University of Virginia (more than anyone else in the history of the school), and after gaining an endowed chair and winning the most prestigious teaching awards on campus, it is self-evident that Ken has the respect of the academic community. He has not had to compromise his faith or convictions and has even had a significant platform to articulate his faith and care for students. Ken has been a fixed point for thousands of students at "Mr. Jefferson's University," one of the most proudly secular campuses in the country.

Unfortunately, one of the most common perceptions and accusations about Christians in general is our hypocrisy and self-righteousness. We tell people and even want to legislate for people how to live right, but don't live right ourselves. In recent years there have been prominent pastors and congressmen who have preached against homosexuality but have been "outed" by their own sexual indiscretions. How do we become a fixed point without becoming rigidly self-righteous?

Self-righteousness is not a new phenomenon. The Pharisees were known for their efforts at righteous living, but Jesus called them "white-washed tombs." The great temptation and danger of highly dedicated people in almost any religion and profession is to be so concerned for perfection that it is impossible to live up to their own standards. This is at the heart of the moral consciousness that C. S. Lewis talks about in *Mere Christianity*. No one can live up to his or her own professed standards, and this seems especially true among those who trumpet standards for others.

So belonging to God cannot be a point of pride or superiority. Rather it needs to be a relationship of gratitude and humility. Then our interior world can better shape our outside, organizational world.

BELONGING TO EACH OTHER

But we also are to belong to each other. Four times Jesus prays that his disciples, that we, would be one—which leaves no doubt as to the importance of his request. And no doubt we do not need to be convinced of the importance of Christian unity. We know that Jesus gave his followers a new commandment—that we "love one another" (Jn 13:34). We know that the apostle Paul exhorts us to make "every effort to maintain the unity of the Spirit" (Eph 4:3). Yet we also know the tensions we can have with each other—not because we necessarily dislike others but probably because others are unlike us.

From a human standpoint it is often difficult to embrace someone else's style of leadership. We gravitate to those who are more like us in temperament, background and social standing. We get embarrassed or defensive about our faith when other believers express their faith differently or don't agree with us about an interpretation of the Bible. We don't want to associate with them.

In his significant study *Faith in the Halls of Power*, Michael Lindsay reached a troubling conclusion about Christian leaders. Many of them—in all fields, whether business, politics, the professions or the academy—do not find close association with a local church to be of much value or help to them in their vocational lives. They feel badgered for money or flattered for their reputation and power, but don't feel that they belong in church.

Although some of this is understandable and perhaps to some degree unavoidable, the net result is that executives and people of

influence in the world are often isolated from others in the body
of Christ outside of their own social networks. There is not a
healthy sense of belonging to those who are not leaders or those
who are less fortunate in terms of abilities and opportunities. As
leaders we cannot isolate ourselves from other believers in either
theory or practice.

Unfortunately, the history of the church is a tragic testimony
of not only isolation but of schisms, splits and actual armed conflict. One of the reasons the philosopher René Descartes formu-
lated his bedrock statement of secular belief, "I think, therefore
I am," was his experience in the Catholic army fighting Protes-
tants during the Thirty Years War. He asked what value the
Christian faith has if it leads to killing others of supposedly the
same faith. He found his own rational thinking processes far
more satisfactory in explaining life's meaning than the irrational
destructiveness of church power.

Centuries later, we may readily critique both Descartes' idolatry of rationality as well as the equally idolatrous power struggles
of church leaders. But those power struggles continue with not
only swords, such as in the Rwandan genocides, but the way we
fight each other with words. Hate speech is frequently associated
with religious fundamentalists, while sarcasm and belittlement
are often the verbal weapons of choice of those of us so convinced
of the rightness of our position.

The issue at stake though, is not really whether we compromise our convictions but whether we compromise Christ's commandment. Christian unity is so significant in the eyes of Christ
that it is identified as a means by which others will come to know
him as the one sent from the Father. Jesus prayed to the Father
for our unity "so that the world may believe that you have sent
me" (Jn 17:21).

One reason we struggle with belonging to one another in the
body of Christ is our own pride. We easily become jealous of the

success of others. This may express itself in criticizing others or of promoting ourselves instead. Either way, we create separation, because as Mary declared in her Magnificat, God scatters the proud.

Human pride in any form leads to fragmentation. By way of contrast, the liberating and healing message of the gospel is that "there is no longer Jew or Greek, there is no longer slave or free, there is no longer male and female; for all of [us] are one in Christ Jesus" (Gal 3:28). Pride produces separateness, but belonging yields and is a deep expression of oneness.

BELONGING IN THE WORLD

We belong to God, we belong to each other, and we belong in the world. Just as the depth of our belonging to God affects the breadth of our belonging to each other, so our oneness affects our life and witness in all dimensions of the world around us.

In the New Testament, *world* occasionally refers to the material universe, the creation. Paul speaks to the Athenians in Acts 17 of "the God who made the world." Just by being alive we are in the physical world. This is a major reason for us to be involved as leaders in environmental stewardship. We are created beings. In *Chariots of Fire*, Eric Liddell exclaimed, "When I run I feel God's pleasure." We too can feel God's pleasure by joyfully being a part of his creation. As Irenaeus said in the second century, "The glory of God is a person fully alive."

A second meaning of *world*, though, has strong "spiritual battle" connotations. It describes the forces of evil and those who are in opposition to God. We are not to belong to this world that is characterized by violence, cynicism and a rejection of God's authority, a world that worships the material rather than the eternal. In fact, Peter describes us as "aliens and exiles." We are to be in the world but we must not be of the world that rebels against God and his purposes.

And this leads to a third meaning of *world*. It refers to the human race, a social world, people that God created and loves. We are clearly to be in *this* world. There can be little misunderstanding of Christ's prayer. He not only acknowledges that his disciples were in the world but he strongly asserts that he was intentionally sending them (and us) into this world.

Our God is a sending God. He is a centrifugal being, always reaching out to his creation. In Genesis 3:9 he asks the man in the Garden, "Where are you?" In 2 Chronicles 16:9 we read, "For the eyes of the LORD range throughout the entire earth, to strengthen those whose heart is true to him." John records forty-two times in his Gospel that Jesus was sent into the world.

Specifically, in John 17 Jesus prays that just as we are to be like the Father and the Son in our unity, we are to be like them in our understanding of being sent. He announces to his disciples "As the Father has sent me, so send I you." An integral part of our calling as believers is to be a part of God's mission in the world despite its evils and temptations. Flannery O'Connor wrote, "If you are a Christian you have to cherish the world at the same time you struggle to endure it."

And this brings me to the core issue. If we belong to God and we belong to each other, and if we belong in the world without being of the world, what does it mean to be sent into the world as Christ was sent into the world?

Obviously, first we are sent to our families, our friends and our neighbors. These are our natural relationships for our life and witness. A fascinating aspect of Jesus' ministry is that he didn't go out to do evangelism. Instead sinners kept coming to him. Why? One reason was that he ate with them. His discipleship community was not so tight that he couldn't share meals with unbelievers. They evidently liked being with him. He didn't live in isolation.

Sometimes we lose our ability to connect in friendship with those around us because ironically we are trying to have "God's heart for the world." Although this desire is commendable, it is not really possible, and we can be so possessed by our vision that we become presumptuous and lose track of that fundamental command to love our neighbor. John Perkins once said that "Only God so loved the world. Our responsibility is to love those around us."

Second, we are to be in the world in terms of our vocational calling. How we do our work and why we do our work is as important as what our work is. How we lead others also communicates the calling of God in our lives. We cannot live in isolation from our Christian commitments and calling.

Tragically that has not always been the posture of large segments of the church. Garrison Keillor humorously writes about his young adult experience, "Truth, such as the doctrine of Separation from the World was appealing to those of us with no social skills—if people didn't like us, it was proof of our righteousness." A similar sentiment is expressed in the old Bible camp chorus "Some folks think that we're peculiar, but we're saved, hallelujer!"

By way of contrast, in *Walking on Water* Madeleine L'Engle writes, "To be a witness means to live in such a way that one's life would not make sense if God did not exist." I believe this gets to the heart of our paradox. We are to be a sign of contradiction in the world, while at the same time, not withdrawing from the world.

This leads to a third sphere of witness in response to the Great Commission of Jesus. We are not only called to our family, friends and professional world, we are also called to be witnesses in a global context. Whether or not we are missionaries or support missionaries, we are to be involved with the mission of God in the world.

So the answer to how to be in the world but not of it relates to our sense of belonging; our belonging to God, our belonging to each other and our belonging in the world. It is a combination of holiness, oneness and sentness.

Finally, there are the two verses that are like bookends to Jesus' prayer in John 17. Chapter 16 ends with Jesus' exhortation, "Take courage; I have conquered the world!" It is a strong message of victory and hope. For us to be effective in our witness in the world we must be people of hope, because the God to whom we belong is a God of hope.

Then at the end of Jesus' prayer, chapter 18 begins with the statement that Jesus went to a garden—the Garden of Gethsemane—a place of humility and suffering. True Christian hope is never a self-centered triumphalism. It is always interpreted by humility. When Jesus came into the world as the Messiah, he came as a baby born in a manger. When he entered into Jerusalem with shouts of *Hosanna*, he was on a donkey, and when he was finally and rightfully addressed as king of the Jews, he was on his cross of shame. At some time in the future, every knee shall bow and every tongue confess that the one who is the Lion of the tribe of Judah is the one who was also the sacrificial Lamb of God.

So going into the world as witnesses for Christ with a sense of superiority will sound to others like a noisy gong or clashing symbols. For us to be in the world captured by our own personal struggles will have little impact on people in despair. But when we live in the world with our hope in Christ and with the humility of Christ, it enables us to live in this world as witnesses for Christ. For Jesus is the one who sends us on this wonderfully paradoxical mission of being in the world but not of it.

TRANSFORMED FROM LONELINESS

The leadership ellipse can also illustrate our loneliness in leadership: the focal point of our interior life is boredom while the focal point of our exterior life is overwork. When we practice an intentional belonging to God, to each other and in the world, we experience a transformation from our loneliness into a more vibrant and peaceful sense of our calling. Jesus' prayerful promise for our belonging becomes a new dynamic in our leadership ellipse.

In a Fragmented World

The Pursuit of Shalom

*Shalom is the substance of the biblical vision
of community embracing all creation.*

WALTER BRUEGGEMANN

In a previous job, I was the supervisor of a very talented but stressed-out woman. I met with her one Friday afternoon and heard how discouraged she was with her work. She expressed a desire to do something different that would be more energizing. I tried to be sympathetic and responded that it might be good for her to do something else. I prayed with her and left for the weekend.

I was then dismayed on Monday morning when I heard from someone else that this colleague was telling others that I had fired her on Friday by encouraging her to consider other avenues of work. I also discovered that she had engaged another woman to be a third party to mediate her improper termination.

Several weeks later after many hours of meetings with the help of the third party, we came to the agreement that I had not fired her but had seriously miscommunicated with her. In a classic male-female difference I had heard the facts of her discontent and had responded with a solution, while what she had wanted was for me to hear her emotional discontent and be supportive of her. She then didn't hear my attempts to help but assumed I was responding to her purely from a position of power. Fortunately, she was able to make a healthy transition to another business, and we are now good friends again. But looking back, I wish I had been more in touch with my own needs and taken the time and emotional energy to listen to her more carefully that late Friday afternoon.

This one vignette represents what happens daily to us as leaders in our churches and organizations. We have good intentions but are not able to avoid interpersonal tensions that often lead to fractured relationships. Even with mature communication skills we sometimes just don't get it. What can we learn that helps us navigate these perplexing tensions among those around us? Let me suggest a broader and deeper understanding of what might be happening.

UNITY AND DIVERSITY

Francis Collins is an extraordinary leader. He successfully led the incredibly complex Human Genome Project with both scientific and organizational brilliance. He also is a dedicated and articulate Christian who writes in his book *The Language of God* that at the DNA level of detail, all humans are "99.9% identical" no matter where in the world we come from. He says that his study of genomes "leads inexorably to the conclusion that we humans share a common ancestor."

This research is consistent with the wisdom that we are not only all very similar in terms of our biological identity but that we have similar psychological and spiritual patterns. We all have fears and hopes, longings and regrets. We all have, in John Calvin's words, "a sense of divinity" or as Pascal declared, we all have a "heart-shaped vacuum" that only God can fill.

These discoveries and observations all give evidence that humans are created by God and in his image. Our existence is not one of random chance but intimate crafting by a relational God. In Psalm 8, David speaks of the glory and honor that God gave to his human creation. The noted Lutheran scholar H. C. Leupold translates the reference to men and women in verse 5 of that Psalm as "thou didst make him [them] lack little of God." The reason God condemned murder in Genesis 9:6 is that it is an act against one who bears the image of God.

Yet despite all of this biological and spiritual sameness, we live in a fractured and broken world. People lament that the world is broken, that the government is broken, that our financial institutions are broken, that families are broken and that the church is broken. There is tremendous fear and insecurity as well as even hatred toward those who in some way are different. Men abuse women, and women ridicule men. Majorities oppress minorities, and the world sees no end to ethnic and religious conflicts.

Why is this so? Why is something that seems so right and valuable so difficult to obtain? Why do issues of race so often end up in various forms of hostility or avoidance? Why is there still the "battle of the sexes" in the workplace and in the church? Why do we continually fight over political differences, and why are so many committee meetings fraught with tension?

In seeking to grapple with these questions I go back to the metaphor of two tributaries flowing into a river. The first tributary in this scenario is the stream of cultural differences that flows with a powerful current of deep and often intangible identity issues. The second is the polluting stream of human sinfulness that muddies and poisons so many of our relationships and organizational experiences.

These tributaries pour into the river of our personal and organizational lives. But instead of merging into a pleasant stream they create turbulent rapids that challenge our spiritual and organizational leadership. We cannot ignore or minimize our cultural differences, but we need to understand and appreciate them. Neither can we avoid the distorting influences of our human sinfulness but we need to face it, confess it and live in new ways.

CULTURAL DIFFERENCES

A major and dominating reason for our struggles is that gender, racial and almost all cultural differences are extremely complex. Sociologist Terry Eagleton says, "Culture is said to be one of the two or three most complex words in the English language." As testimony of this the Willowbank Report defines culture as "an integrated system of beliefs, of values, of customs and of institutions . . . which bind a society together and give it a sense of dignity, security and continuity. . . . Culture is the patterned way in which people do things together." Sometimes in business circles we say that our corporate culture "is the way we do things around here."

This means though that culture not only defines what something is but also excludes what it is not. We do something a certain way, which means we don't do it another way. Some cultures luxuriate in the passing of time, while others are driven to maximize time. A high-church culture is restrained in its expression of worship, while a Pentecostal culture is far more demonstrative. Some women thrive on being a stay-at-home mom, while others thrive in a professional work setting; many others try to do both. We often define who we are by who we are not.

But what makes culture so powerful is that it often functions at the subconscious level. We don't think we speak with an accent until we meet people who do. Because of our natural cultural blinders, we cannot presume to know what others experience from different family or educational backgrounds. This is especially true with respect to race or ethnic diversity. Our racial identity is deeply embedded in us through the cultural signals we receive from family, schools, churches, the media and our vocational environments. We live in a sea of cultural diversity.

Consequently, it is important to have a common understanding of cultural differences if we hope to understand and live with them. Although there are many ways of segmenting and analyzing culture, let me suggest three broad categories that illustrate the varied cultural influences in both our individual and corporate lives.

Inherited cultures. The first and most general category of influence is made up of what we have inherited genetically through our parents. We are born as either men or women with a certain skin pigmentation and defining physical characteristics. We are one of more that thirty-five hundred ethnicities in the world that continue to expand through interethnic marriages.

In addition to our physical appearance we also inherit our intellectual capacities, our temperament and our personality characteristics. We may seek to change what we are through hard work or surgery (or denial), but there is so much that we can't change. We are who we are, and we are all uniquely different.

Alice and I have two daughters three years apart in age that look very much alike, sound alike, have the same Myers-Briggs pattern, and were raised in the same home and school environment. Yet they are different people in their motivations, their gifts and how they live. They are clearly sisters in external characteristics, but uniquely different people internally.

Because we can't change them, our inherited cultures are the most powerful influence on how we relate to others in our lives. This is especially powerful in matters of race and gender because these differences are so immediately and physically obvious. Consequently, inherited cultural differences are the most common cause for prejudice and conflict. It is easier to dismiss a whole group of people than to get to know any of them individually.

Absorbed cultures. A second major cultural pattern is what we unconsciously absorb in our life experiences. It includes those influences that come naturally in our experiences of growing up. Nationality, language, religious experience and communal ethnicity are all part of this absorbed cultures. This level of culture frequently modifies our inherited cultures.

A good example is President Barack Obama. He inherited both black Kenyan and white Kansas genes. There is no doubt he is African American. But he has also clearly absorbed international sensitivities and cultural influences from his childhood years in Hawaii and Indonesia. The urban cultures from his time in New York and Chicago have also contributed to who he is.

Another example is missionary children who were born and raised in a foreign culture but often have great difficulties adjusting to American culture even though they are legally Americans. Second- and third-generation Asian Americans have similar problems when they visit the birth country of their parents or grandparents. They may have a Korean heritage and look Korean, but they may not speak Korean or even feel quite at home in Korea.

This process by which we absorb our natural surrounding culture is called enculturation, and it is part of all our lives. Enculturation is what enables families and ethnic groups to pass along their values and traditions to succeeding generations. It includes food preferences, styles of music, work habits and ways of handling conflict. The stronger the enculturation process, the stronger the person's cultural identity is.

However, this identity, which is a great source of security and comfort in a monocultural setting, can abruptly result in tensions in a work environment made up of those with different cultural patterns. A common example is dealing with conflict. Western cultures are often described as guilt-based in contrast with Eastern cultures that are more shame-based. A guilt-based culture is a win-lose culture characterized by direct conflict, while a shame-based culture tries to save face and discuss difficult issues indirectly or through a third party.

Such tensions are not only part of ethnic and gender differences, but also of generational differences. Churches and workplaces struggle to create an effective and collaborative working community made up of baby boomers that have absorbed a culture of workaholism and those of younger generations who treat work differently. So someone from the boomer generation may take work home while a twenty-something colleague may rather go to a movie with friends. All forms of enculturation have an effect on working relationships.

Learned cultures. Although they may be closely linked with absorbed cultures, learned cultures are usually the result of conscious choices. For instance, a student may choose a residential college educational system which is a different culture than most high school educational experiences. So a student needs to choose to learn how to study in order to feel comfortable in an academic environment. Similarly, we choose to learn an organizational culture that is different from the culture of our family or friendship network. Farm people have to learn urban or suburban culture to work in a metropolitan area, while city folks may need to learn small-town culture if they choose a less intense lifestyle.

Learned cultures are necessary in a world of rapid transportation and instant communication. Yet they are detached and feel uncomfortable in comparison with inherited and absorbed cultures, unless they are reinforced by those cultures. So, first-generation college students are more likely to experience the culture shock of college life than those whose parents went to college.

But even at college there are cultural differences, like between those in different departments on campus. In the novel *New England White*, Stephen Carter writes about those in the economics tower looking "condescendingly down on the superstitious rabble" of the divinity school. He goes on to comment, "the one where truth was measurable but not eternal, the other where truth was eternal but not measurable." I get the sense that Yale professor Carter is not speaking in a totally fictitious way!

But this is true in other arenas of endeavor as well. In business the culture of the accounting department is different from the sales department, and the culture of a major corporation is different from that of a local business. Likewise parachurch ministry is a crosscultural experience for those from churches who have not had that tradition.

Similarly, multiethnic cultures are learned cultures themselves. It is likely to be uncomfortable for everyone to become a part of them. Even knowing whether to clap on the first or second beats of a song is culturally determined and awkward to learn, but especially if you try to incorporate both rhythms at once! Healthy cultural diversity is not natural but has to be learned, and the best way to do this is through intentional and honest conversations and shared experiences.

At InterVarsity Press, we have worked at doing this through some ethnic-specific author consultations as well as a multiethnic job fair. In these events we introduce the outside participants to the various aspects of publishing but then solicit their input for our learning benefit. These occasions have been mutually beneficial opportunities to learn what kinds of books are most needed in each ethnic community and how to design and promote them most effectively.

Inherited, absorbed and learned cultures all add to the differences we experience with each other. But differences are not intrinsically bad. Like steel or other alloys that are stronger than their pure metals, diversity in human groupings brings a breadth and strength of understanding and performance.

However, the ingredient that takes all of these differences and makes them destructive rather than synergistically valuable is the subterranean effect of our human sinfulness.

HUMAN SINFULNESS

Despite the idyllic state of Eden, disobedience to God fractured the relationship between God and his human creation. Isaiah 59:2 proclaims that our sins "have been barriers between you and your God." Like Adam and Eve, we not only experience separation from God but from creation. We feel cursed in our labors and experience enmity between each other as women and men.

Also like Cain and Abel, we have fractured relationships between family members. We experience interpersonal tension in our churches and in our jobs. We engage in collective strife through tribal conflicts, ethnic hostilities and global wars. We live in a fractured world.

The apostle James answers his rhetorical question, "What causes wars?" with the clear declaration that it is the sin within us. The noted church historian Martin Marty puts it another way when he says that the world is not really divided between liberals and conservatives, but between "mean and non-mean" people.

There are many all too familiar and overwhelming examples of how sin is fracturing our world on a daily basis. We abhor the arrogance and human destruction of genocide and war in distant places, but also experience the pain of divorce and slander and abuses in our own families and working relationships. We have this external preening of spiritual unity or political correctness, but like the peacock we have a strident cry that betrays the ugliness of our meager hearts.

Sometimes our sinfulness is like permafrost in arctic lands. Because the winters are so cold, the ground is always frozen eighteen inches or more below the surface. Consequently tree roots cannot go deeper and the upward growth of the trees is stunted. In a parallel way, if the core of our hearts is frozen toward those different from us, we never will have deep experiences of reconciliation, and our capacity for peace and harmony will never grow.

But if the fundamental cause to our problems is not our differences but our sinfulness, how do we solve these problems? Do we pray and hope for the best? We may be suspicious of this approach since mere personal piety seems to have little affect in dealing with major issues of injustice. Slavery was sanctioned and justified by many pious pastors and church leaders. The reason the exhortation to "just pray about it" is frequently insufficient is because our prayers too often reflect and reinforce the hardness of our hearts rather being the means of prompting us to action.

However, if piety alone is not the answer, what is? Does social activism always lead to justice? Does sensitivity training remove attitudes of superiority or simply hide them? If we are followers of Jesus in a fractured world, what can we do that has spiritual authenticity and practical impact? We need to deal with both our internal sinfulness and the external manifestations of sin. We need to follow the path of shalom.

THE PATH OF SHALOM

Shalom is a Hebrew word that is often translated as "peace" in the Old Testament. It is used as a greeting or it can refer to a desire for social justice. It has social, ethical and spiritual dimensions. Perry Yoder says, "Shalom sometimes refers to material and physical conditions, sometimes to relationships and sometimes to moral behavior. In all three of these arenas, shalom defines how things should be." The psalmist says, "Depart from evil, and do good; / seek peace [shalom], and pursue it." Shalom is the antidote to our fragmented and fractured relationships. It brings healing and harmony. It is a call to reconciliation in all of our relationships.

Shalom is a word and value that is also used in a broader sociological and cultural way. The prophet Jeremiah wrote to the people of Israel who were captive in pagan Babylon about how they should live. Instead of instigating insurrection, Jeremiah encourages them to "seek the welfare [shalom] of the city . . . and pray to the LORD on its behalf" (Jer 29:7). I believe it is appropriate to apply this instruction to all of our social and institutional relationships. We should seek the shalom of our churches, our businesses, our communities, our country and our world, and we do this through both our actions and the testimony of our character. Isaiah 32:17 says, "The effect of righteousness will be peace."

In the New Testament the apostle Paul is very explicit in identifying that Jesus "is our peace" and that he has "broken down the dividing wall" of hostility between not only Jews and Gentiles but among all peoples. Paul prays for our "shalom" and then tells us that this God of peace has entrusted to us this message of reconciliation and peace (see Eph 2). Ultimately this is the peace that comes through the death and resurrection of Jesus but it is to be demonstrated by the peace of God "ruling in our hearts." Our internal spiritual health affects our ability to pursue the path of shalom. Jesus is the Prince of Peace, and as we follow him in steps of faithfulness we too should seek to bring shalom to everything we touch.

Although there are unlimited needs for shalom in our fragmented world, I would like to address two of the most general and difficult points of fracture that challenge our leadership effectiveness. They are the need for greater gender equality and racial reconciliation in all of our churches, institutions and relationships.

GENDER SHALOM

Ever since Adam and Eve there has been tension between the sexes. Even though men and women were made for each other and we experience our most intimate and satisfying expressions of human love with each other, there are all too many times when we don't connect well with each other which results in fractured relationships and dissolved marriages. Unfortunately Christian faith does not seem to make much difference, as divorce levels for Christians and those who are not Christians are pretty much the same. In fact, the different theological convictions within the church about women in leadership often add another dimension of conflict.

The situation in the marketplace is not any better. Although schools and companies are required by law to not discriminate between men and women with respect to salaries and promotions, there is still a great deal of sexism in the workplace as well as in the church. Women are victims of or suspicious of gender bias when bad things happen to them, and men are resentful when women who may or may not be more qualified are promoted ahead of them to achieve a better gender balance. How do we lead from the inside out in ways that bring peace to these conflicts and tensions?

The issues of gender identity and equality are often far deeper and more personal than can be solved by laws or generic principles. Our sexuality touches the very core of our being and is strongly shaped by our family of origin experiences. Abuse, neglect, affirmations and opportunities are all part of who we are and how much we respect or decry our gender differences. When we have had healthy gender relationships in our families and institutions, we are much more resilient and less accusatory of others when gender dynamics are flawed. When our experiences have been difficult we are fearful of damaging patterns happening again.

So one foundational response to fractured gender relationships is a humble spirit and not quickly categorizing a person or their actions into a gender stereotype. There are often many reasons apart from gender differences that affect a person's decisions. Careful listening and giving the benefit of the doubt are social graces that can bring shalom to a conflict situation.

Daughters of Zelophehad. Not all gender-related problems, though, can be solved by good relationships. Sometimes there are policies and practices that are gender-biased and need to be changed. A great biblical example of this occurs twice in the book of Numbers. The first introduces us to five daughters of a leader of the tribe of Manasseh, Zelophehad. He died without a son to receive his inheritance. According to the Mosaic Law, this inheritance was to be distributed to the broader family instead of to his daughters, as women were not allowed to receive such an inheritance.

The daughters did not think this was right and raised this question with Moses, who brought it before the Lord in Numbers 27. Remarkably the Lord agreed with the daughters and instructed Moses to divide the inheritance among them. This was a change from Hebrew patriarchal traditions but a wonderful illustration of people in authority (including the Lord!) listening to the legitimate complaints of a powerless group of people and doing something for them. Moses must have been very secure in his inner self to take that outer risk of leadership.

But as often is the case in "policy changes," the solution created different problems. What was fair to the daughters felt unfair to their kinsmen. As recorded in Numbers 36, the family heads of Manasseh were concerned that the daughters might marry outside of their tribe and take Zelophehad's inheritance with them. Since the inheritance was tied in with land, they as a tribe would then collectively lose land to another tribe.

So these leaders brought their request to Moses, who went to the Lord a second time, and the Lord changed the policy again. The final ruling was that the daughters would still receive the inheritance, but they had to marry within their tribe. This would keep the appropriate balance of territorial power between the tribes while also honoring the rights of the five daughters. This then becomes the concluding command for the Israelites in the book of Numbers.

What is fascinating to me in this story is how practical and open the discussions and decisions are. The daughters had an appropriate grievance against a sexist practice. They took it to their leader, Moses, who saw it as both an organizational and spiritual matter.

Although I wish I knew how Moses and the Lord could dialogue so clearly about this, I am encouraged to know that the Lord does care about these kinds of policies and decisions. Shalom came to these daughters and their tribe because of good practical and evolving decisions. The path of gender shalom requires attentive listening, flexibility, compromise and intentional actions.

A good way to get better at this is to have a trained outside facilitator meet with your leadership team to discuss these issues. Another option is to lead your team in discussing a book like MaryKate Morse's *Making Room for Leadership: Power, Space and Influence*. In this book Morse notes that many if not most women regularly experience attitudes and actions from others that challenge their equality and sense of significance. She then introduces many profitable insights for greater interpersonal awareness, discussion and cultural change.

RACIAL SHALOM

When I was in my last year in college my senior project partner, Phil, was from Baltimore and African American. I am of a very mixed European ethnic background. We worked well together and seemed to be good friends. One week, though, right in the middle of our most intense time of working on our project, Phil didn't show up for class. At first I thought he was sick, but he wasn't at his apartment.

Because I was left stuck with all the work, I felt quite resentful toward Phil until our professor told me that Phil had gone home because his mother had just been killed by a stray bullet from a gang war in their neighborhood. It was then I realized that I did not really know Phil and the difficult circumstances and pressures that were an intrinsic part of his life. When Phil came back to school, I tried to talk with him, but the pain he was enduring was far greater than I could understand or he could discuss.

Since that time I have become more and more aware of how unequal we all are with respect to culture and especially race. Those of us in a majority culture situation are so often unaware of how much our majority status gives us privilege and power wherever we go. By way of contrast, those from a minority cultural background have continual life experiences that openly question and challenge their legitimacy and identity.

So as either minority or majority leaders, we must listen to others and also get in touch with what is happening inside of ourselves. Although diversity training is often ridiculed and avoided, it can be very helpful. It is good to know how others respond to us apart from our own perceptions. For instance, InterVarsity's board of trustees discussed George Yancey's *Beyond Racial Gridlock: Embracing Mutual Responsibility* as a way for a multiethnic board to better understand each other's assumptions and concerns.

But training in itself does not get at the core issues that hinder shalom in our lives. This is why being attentive to our own hearts and minds allows for us to be in better touch with others. It also allows us to hope, and hope is an intrinsic part of Christian faith. Kathryn McGready says, "hope is the memory of the future," and ultimately our hope is in God and not in human institutions or social structures. Our hope is in God's redemptive work being done in us. The challenge for us as leaders is to provide the commitment and the organizational climate that promotes and facilitates racial reconciliation and shalom in a spirit of hope.

Honoring one another. One foundational principle and attitude in pursuing a path of racial shalom is the practice of honoring everybody as being made in the image of God. There are no superior or inferior races or ethnicities, and we demonstrate this conviction not by a minimalistic tolerance but by the biblical ethic of honor. "Honor your father and your mother" (Ex 20:12) is part of the Ten Commandments. Paul teaches us to honor the governor (Rom 13:1-7) and to honor one another (Rom 12:10). Psalm 8:5

says that God gave glory and honor to his creation and this will be manifested in heaven when the honor of all the nations will be displayed (Rev 21:26). The implication is that there is a unique richness in ethnic diversity to be recognized and enjoyed. So we should honor all aspects of what God has given to us in our humanity including our ethnicity.

Practically speaking, honor means a total rejection of racist attitudes and actions. It means not ignoring others because of their gender or ethnicity. Honor means respect for a person and for their cultural heritage. Honor means making sure that minorities have recognition and advancement and organizational power. Honoring one another is a command of God.

Offering ourself. It is also important to offer ourself to others. Spiritually, we do this by offering confession for our own sins and, when necessary, the sins of others. Whether consciously or unconsciously we are all guilty of the sin of intolerance and of racism—of not loving our neighbors as we do ourselves. Scripture is clear that both intentional and unintentional sins need to be confessed (Lev 4:27-28). The same is true for corporate sin (Lev 4:13-14). Shalom is the "way things ought to be" and this is the path of confession.

A corollary to offering confession is offering forgiveness. Christ came to save us from our guilt and sin. As we offer forgiveness, we share in the divine work of redemption. The principles of the Old Testament cities of refuge taught that there was safety for unintentional sin and that there was a time limitation for holding a grudge against another (Deut 19:1-14). Our places of work need to be places of refuge characterized by a spirit of forgiveness.

Practicing confession and forgiveness is never easy but is even more difficult in racial matters when there may be long-standing suspicions or hurts. Consequently there is no formula or checklist to be completed. Confession and forgiveness aren't something to be done in a perfunctory manner or with the assumption that "we can now move on." My experience is that we need to live an integrity of confession and forgiveness that comes from our inner character and is a continual practice. Just as we are called to offer ourself to God on a daily basis, so we are to offer ourself to one another in a spirit of humility and trust.

Practicing reconciliation. In addition to these spiritual values there are the regular problems and misunderstandings that require conscious reconciliation. One particular area of confusion and conflict for different cultures is in the area of authority. Western cultural traditions are highly individualistic and have spawned capitalism, democracy and a deeply ingrained, highly cherished value of independence. This not only affects our political realm but our churches and workplaces as well. The university world tenaciously embraces a fierce individuality, and the Internet has further multiplied this democratization of not only information but authority as well.

Yet not all cultures view and practice authority in this manner. Many still hold to an authoritarian form of leadership. This creates a complex and confusing situation when minorities with a strong hierarchical view of authority become part of a more egalitarian work environment.

As an example, it has often been the experience of black leaders who are welcomed into largely white organizations to find that they don't have the respect or leadership power they have in their black congregations or organizations. For most ethnic minority groups, power flows from the top down, but many white organizations work hard at practicing power from the bottom up. I know of white pastors who are jealous of the power and respect that black pastors receive from their congregations.

For any church or organization to have a healthy multicultural dynamic, there needs to be honest discussion and agreement on the roles of power and authority, because a truly multicultural organization is a new culture in itself, which is probably uncomfortable for everyone in some way.

A WAY OF PEACE

The path of shalom is difficult but desperately needed in a fractured world. It is a way of peace and reconciliation that provides healing and demonstrates the power of the gospel to overcome divisions and conflicts in the world. It is not a path of homogenization but rather of harmonization. It is our privilege and calling as leaders to lead others into an experience of shalom that is characterized by difference rather than dissonance. This may be our greatest witness to a broken world longing for healing and wholeness, and it comes from who we are as leaders before God and others.

PART THREE

SHAPING OUR
LEADERSHIP

As More Than a Grasshopper

The Practice of Wholeheartedness

A spy is one who penetrates into a hidden mystery,
and a spy of God is one who sees at the
heart of every manifestation of life . . .
the mysterium tremendum *that is God.*

HELEN LUKE

There is a fascinating psychological and spiritual leadership dynamic that occurs in a story about the Israelites in the thirteenth chapter of the book of Numbers. The situation is that Moses had sent out twelve handpicked, top-flight leaders from among the Israelites to explore the land that God had promised to give to them. He instructed them to evaluate the soil conditions, vegetation and to take note of what the people were like. They were a blue-ribbon group of leaders and advisers to Moses.

When they returned from their reconnaissance, the majority confessed great fear of the land's inhabitants: "We are not able to go up against these people, for they are stronger than we" (Num 13:31). These are the same people and leaders who had recently experienced miracle after miracle as God led them out of Egypt and protected them from Pharaoh's army. But they no longer believed in either their strength or the power of their God.

The most revealing statement in their report though is not just their assessment of military inferiority but this astonishing admission: "to ourselves we seemed like grasshoppers, and so we seemed to them" (Num 13:33). Unlike the image of a peacock that portrays a commanding sense of presence, the grasshopper is an irritating, destructive insect. It is not something to look at with admiration but is something that needs to be swatted away. These senior leaders must have been really scared to admit that they felt like grasshoppers. Leaders don't admit such feelings of inferiority.

But with their self-deprecation comes the remarkable awareness that their small view of themselves also affected their perception of how others perceived them. They reinforced their own fear by their assumptions of what others thought of them.

What causes this kind of fear? Is it just a lack of faith and courage that makes leaders timid? Do we need continual exhortations in vision casting and confidence in God to get "our rear in gear"? What does it take to be like Joshua and Caleb, who were the minority report and wanted to take the land?

Let me suggest that although strong spiritual commitment and faith in God are foundational for effective Christian leadership, this state of genuine confidence does not come from just revving ourself up through motivational talks and techniques. In fact the need for such external stimulation indicates that there are bigger (giant!) issues in our lives that inhibit our holy boldness. What are these giants that strike fear into our leadership? Let me suggest three giants that challenge our spiritual psyche and make us feel like grasshoppers in our own eyes and in the eyes of others.

The Giant of Failure

Failure for most of us is a messy and traumatic realization that something has gone wrong in our life. For some it is a failed marriage. For others it is a failed parenting, failed relationships or failure in our Christian devotion. We experience guilt and regret, and try to move on. But our most debilitating times of failure are usually connected with job loss, because our identity is so strongly associated with our work. We are proud of what we do and what we accomplish. When we lose our role, for whatever reason, we become disoriented in who we are. We often feel defensive or inadequate or both.

Urban myth suggests that leadership development is a smooth climb up the corporate, ecclesiastical or academic ladder, but the reality is that most leaders experience small, medium and sometimes significant disappointment if not outright failure in our leadership. The experience of job failure is very public and accepted in the world of sports, where baseball managers and football coaches are regularly hired and fired. Some of the best leaders in the sports world have been fired many times—even by the same organization!

But we are not so casual if we are a pastor and we are asked to leave the church that we have founded or have served faithfully for many years. Nor are we eager for family and friends to know that the company has been reorganized or downsized, and we are asked to take or find another job.

Even in the tenured world of academics, we lament the time when our institutional role is weakened through administrative changes or departmental turf wars; or when our reputation in our academic discipline is threatened by harsh and unfair reviews of something we have written. As much as we wish our career would have a constant upward trajectory, virtually all of us have to face the giant of failure. We try to fight the giant through excessive hard work, but when we succumb to the reality of our failure we feel like a grasshopper.

I experienced this in a rather traumatic fashion in the middle of my leadership career. At the time I had been the national director of campus ministries with InterVarsity for fourteen years. This was my dream job because it encompassed my love for students, faculty and the academic world. It was a great leadership challenge to provide effective Christian witness and ministry on hundreds of secular campuses throughout the country. The issues were (and are) enormous, but it was something I felt strongly called to do, and there had been significant growth and success during my tenure.

However, there was a time when the whole organization felt stuck. We had lots of good leaders but our structural arrangements seemed to dilute leadership energy rather than release it. Because we were a highly distributed organization with lots of delegated authority and power, many leaders felt marginalized in their leadership roles.

Consequently, our president decided to reorganize our top structure and eliminate my job, which he absorbed into his job. This was very difficult for me to accept, especially since the decision happened dramatically in the middle of some national meetings that I was leading. My immediate reaction to this loss of my dream job was of great despair and discouragement. Although the president strongly wanted me to stay with the organization in some capacity, I didn't know what my role would be or what my future would look like. My emotions were both a mixture of anger at him and others for making this change so precipitously, as well as a deep sense of personal failure and humiliation. I felt emotionally and professionally crushed.

What was even more devastating was that I didn't know where God was in all of this. I was confused as to whether I had failed God or God had failed me. But either way, I was spiritually confused, frustrated and angry. Was this job loss what I deserved after years of dedication of trying to faithfully serve God? In my despair and emptiness I cried to the Lord for hours for some understanding and comfort. The Lord graciously answered my pleas of desperation with two passages of Scripture.

First, there were the words of Jesus from the cross, "My God, my

God, why have you forsaken me?" (Mt 27:46). When these words spontaneously formed on my lips, I shuddered because they felt blasphemous for me to utter. The experience of losing my job in no way compared to what Jesus suffered in his death. Yet there was also comfort in that what I was experiencing in a very small way was what Jesus had experienced for me. I could trust him as one who had also experienced divine isolation. I was no longer completely alone.

The other passage also included words of Jesus when he prayed for those who were gathered around his place of execution. "Father, forgive them; for they do not know what they are doing" (Lk 23:34). Here was the profound example of Jesus offering forgiveness to those who had rejected him. When I felt most discouraged, without anyone else in the world that understood what was happening to me internally, the Lord gave me his example and encouragement to follow in his steps.

I saw in Jesus a call to let go of my instinctive attitudes of vindictiveness and self-justification. Instead I was to offer forgiveness. Without this quiet invasion of divine grace that day, I think I would have gone down the path of having bitterness against the organization and its leadership. But the path of forgiveness was a road to liberation for me and for how I felt about my colleagues. As Henri Nouwen wisely observed, "forgiveness is allowing the other person not to be God."

This experience may be more or less traumatic than what you have or will experience. Yet, I suspect that this giant of failure or fear of failure does more to disable leadership effectiveness than almost anything else. Facing this giant and believing that there is still milk and honey in what God promises to us is part of the spiritual work that God does within us.

THE GIANT OF SELF-PITY

This may seem like an oxymoron because self-pity is often associated with what is small and insignificant. However, I believe it was

Fred Smith Sr. who used to say, "self-pity is the most dangerous and addictive of all non-pharmaceutical narcotics." This is a strong statement but one that I have observed and experienced to be true even though self-pity is either ignored or dismissed in most leadership literature. Why is this so? Why is such a powerful internal force not addressed? Why don't we talk about it in leadership seminars or among ourselves? Why do we want to skip this section or feel that it doesn't apply to us?

The most obvious reason seems to be that self-pity is so unattractive and debilitating that we don't want to even associate it with leadership. It is like a contagious disease that we don't want to get near. Self-pity falls into the category of sniveling, of whining, of cowardliness and any other pejorative characteristic that defines people who can't lead. We are embarrassed to name it or be identified with it. Self-pity is just not something that we associate with leadership, and it even symbolizes the antithesis of a leadership that is bold, sacrificial, visionary and confident.

But just because we don't like the disease and want to avoid all contact with or mention of it, this doesn't mean that we are not carriers of it or susceptible to its effects on our leadership. In fact the more we try to deny or suppress it, the more it can eat at us internally and weaken both our internal soul and our external leadership.

Because self-pity is such an offensive but private giant, we can even unconsciously shrink back from being faithful to the call of God. Like leprosy, self-pity can be a disease that blinds us and isolates us from others. Self-pity is one of the responses to what we call and experience as positional distance in leadership—when our followers are not the close friends we used to have or that we desperately need to have in our leadership roles.

Another expression of self-pity is the excessive leadership perks and compensation that are ugly for others but are a beautiful temptation for us. We may howl derisively when we hear of the professional athlete and his or her agent demanding a multimillion dollar contract for "what they are worth" without acknowledging that we interpret our salary and our home, car, office and perhaps even something as small as a parking space as "what we are worth."

In a capitalistic environment this mentality works—at least outwardly. We live in a supply and demand culture, and we usually have policies and ways of determining salaries and compensation that attempt to be objective and related to what a person is "worth" in the marketplace. We try to measure this worth according to experience, education, competence and comparisons with others with similar jobs and responsibilities. Although these policies are imperfect and notoriously difficult to administer to everyone's understanding and liking, they are part of our culture.

Let me also add that there are perks and matters of compensation that are directly related to the ability to do our leadership job well. A general in the eighteenth century could not lead his troops well without a horse on which to ride or associates to give him strategic information in the midst of the battle. George Washington was "worth more" with respect to the success of the Continental Army than virtually anyone else in or out of uniform.

Similarly all leaders need resources to lead well, whether these resources are in terms of information, communication, technology, office space, privacy or other items that cost money and time. If we take our leadership responsibilities seriously and care for the people we are called to lead, we are always thinking about them and our job, and we do need and benefit from various perks that help us to be restored and supported physically and emotionally.

So what I am talking about is neither in the category of what we truly need or what may be appropriate to our leadership responsibilities, but what happens inside of us that keeps telling us that no matter what we have, we are worth more and we consequently blame others or our circumstances for our lack of recognition or power or prestige. When we work so hard, we just deserve more!

As I have wrestled with this in my own life, I find that my greatest temptations to self-pity come when my identity issues become distorted. This is especially true when I identify too much with my job role and overly compare myself with others. When I lost my dream job, the reason why it hurt so much was not just that I lost a job but that I lost my identity. This job was how people knew me—not just in InterVarsity but in my church and even in my family. My parents and wife and daughters were proud of me. They were proud of my role. This job was why I was invited to speak at conferences. This job gave me credibility, recognition and power. Losing it felt like a far-too-early retirement. Woe is me. Life wasn't fair and I didn't deserve to be treated this way. This wasn't my fault and I needed to pity myself since no one else was. I felt like a grasshopper in my own eyes and in the perceived eyes of others.

As I struggled with these feelings of despair and self-pity, I thought of Gollum in J. R. R. Tolkien's *Lord of the Rings* trilogy. Here was a creature who was despicable to look at and was consumed with the ring he nauseatingly called "my precious." I read these stories to our daughters when they were young, and when I did so I used the most nasal and irritating voice I could to mimic Gollum's self-infatuating and loathsome possessiveness.

So I was shocked and repulsed when I realized that my job had become "my precious." In the spirit of hard work and company loyalty, I had given my life and soul to my job but at the same time had unconsciously given up my identity apart from my job. What made this so confusing and difficult to see before was that I was a Christian leader who aspired to an all-out dedication to God in my job. I had imbibed the rallying call of "work, for the night is coming" from too many Christian commitment talks—some of which I had given myself!

Yet upon reflection I realized that self-pity has been a tremendous problem for leaders going back to the Old Testament. For instance, the prophet Elijah, even after one of his greatest spiritual and vocational victories, lapsed into self-pity and despair. Elijah had previously stood up to the prophets of Baal in a spectacular display of spiritual chutzpa and courage. He was able to predict droughts; he performed miracles of multiplying food and raising a boy from the dead. He was on his game as a prophet of God. But then in the face of a threat from a powerful woman, Jezebel, he lost it and complained to God, "It is enough; now, O LORD, take away my life," and then a month later, "I alone am left, and they are seeking my life, to take it away" (see 1 Kings 19).

Even Moses, this most remarkable ancient leader, studied and emulated by Alexander the Great for his military strategies, had times of great despair and self-pity. When the people of Israel were getting ready to enter the Promised Land, they started complaining about their limited diet of manna. This made the Lord angry, which sparked great displeasure in Moses. Let me quote at length Moses' complaint to the Lord to communicate the depth of his frustration and self-pity.

> Why have you treated your servant so badly? Why have I not found favor in your sight, that you lay the burden of all this people on me? Did I conceive all this people? Did I give birth to them, that you should say to me, "Carry them in your bosom, as a nurse carries a sucking child," to the land that you promised on oath to their ancestors? Where am I to get meat to give all of these people? For they come weeping to me and say, "Give us meat to eat!" I am not able to carry all this people alone, for they are too heavy for me. If this is the way you are going to treat me, put me to death at once—if I have found favor in your sight—and do not let me see my misery. (Num 11:11-15)

The giant of self-pity was threatening Moses' ability to lead the people.

Yet I don't blame my commitment to God as an excuse for idol-
izing my job role and job identity. Also I don't blame a sense of
Christian evangelistic urgency on my loss of perspective. I have
heard too many business motivational talks to suggest that only
Christian leaders live with this sense of a hyped motivation. The
problem is endemic with all leaders because it is part of our humanity. We pump ourselves up with success and then feel very
empty inside when that success cannot be sustained or is taken
away from us.

GIANT OF EGO AND JEALOUSY

The third giant that undermines our ability to lead with faith
and boldness is comparing ourselves to others in a way that either puffs us up or tears down others. For many men this stereo-
typically manifests itself in aggressive competitiveness that puts
our accomplishments in a better light or trash talks others into a
lesser light. We celebrate the victories of the male ego, but we
also can be destroyed by it when we either lose or try to make
others lose. We manifest the unhealthy parts of the male ego
when we try to dominate, control or criticize others so that we
look better or smarter or more successful. As a daily reminder of
this propensity, I once taped to my desk the observation of the
historian Will Durant, who said, "to speak ill of others is a dishonest way of praising yourself."

For many women the stereotypical dimension of this battle is
jealousy. Sometimes it is jealousy of relationships or of recognition from men and women. Sometimes women are jealous of men
when men seem to be getting preferential treatment or status because of their gender rather than their competence.

My wife once wrote a book on jealousy that is now out of print
because not enough people wanted to read a book that identifies
and unpacks such a private and difficult spiritual battle. Interest-
ingly enough, some years after Alice wrote this book, she was

teaching about classical spiritual struggles, or what some have called "signature sins." As Alice took her teaching to heart, she reluctantly realized that her greatest struggle was with jealousy. She both cried and laughed when she remembered that she had written a whole book about that!

There is a great danger though in assuming gender stereotypes for either ourself or others. Many men struggle with jealousy and many women have ego problems. So it may be better to recognize that ego and jealousy are like two sides of the same coin. Ego is the aggressive, preening side, and jealousy is the hidden, fuming side. Both men and women carry this spiritually debilitating currency no matter which side of the coin is more noticeable.

For instance, Moses was a leader who experienced ego battles but also fought the giant of jealousy. A striking example of this occurred while Moses was organizing the children of Israel for their journey into the Promised Land. It happened right after Moses expressed his death wish that I quoted earlier. In response to Moses' exhaustion and inability to do everything himself, the Lord had told Moses to choose seventy elders and to bring them together to "the tent of meeting." This was one of the first recorded leadership summits, and the Lord used it to teach the principle of delegation. He told Moses that he wanted to take some of the spirit of authority that Moses had and distribute it among the seventy elders so that they could help Moses carry the burden of all the people.

When this happened, the elders prophesied as a manifestation of God's delegated spiritual authority to them. Unfortunately, two of the elders, Eldad and Medad, did not get to the tent of the meeting with all of the others. Yet they too prophesied. This caused some panic among the young men close to Moses who evidently didn't think that Eldad and Medad should be prophesying when they didn't come to the meeting. They went and told Moses which prompted Moses' assistant, Joshua to exclaim, "My lord Moses, stop them!"

At this point Moses insightfully interprets what is happening and exhorts Joshua with the rhetorical question, "Are you jealous for my sake? Would that all of the LORD's people were prophets, and that the LORD would put his spirit on them!" (see Num 11:24-30).

Moses saw that blessing and spiritual authority did not have to be a zero-sum game. This story also uncovers the instinctive motivation in so many of us to protect and defend our spiritual authority and status as leaders. We can be jealous for our own sake, or we can be jealous for the sake of our president or senior pastor or mentor. We like the reflected glory of this important relationship, and we don't want other leaders and especially those who miss the meeting to share it with us.

Jealousy and ego also affect how we gauge our perceived importance in daily organizational life. I remember being stunned to read that cabinet officers to President Richard M. Nixon used a tape measure to see whose office was bigger and whose office was closer to the Oval Office. How petty. However, how many of us have also done the same thing mentally (if not with a tape measure)? If someone is closer to organizational power than we are, we know it and feel it. The challenge is what do we do with that knowledge and those feelings? How do we face down the giant of ego and jealousy?

THE PRACTICE OF WHOLEHEARTEDNESS

Perhaps the best way to deal with this giant, as well as the giants of fear and self-pity, is to follow the example of Caleb, who articulated the minority report of wanting to go into the Promised Land despite the giants. In the midst of the people's agitation over the giants, Caleb quieted the people and said, "Let us go up at once and occupy it" (Num 13:30). Later on in his recollection of this event he humbly said that in response to Moses' request to spy out the land, he "brought [Moses] an honest report" and "wholeheartedly followed the LORD" (Josh 14:7-8).

At a casual glance this description of Caleb seems rather boilerplate for Christian leaders. What is more obvious than the need for honesty and spiritual commitment? Aren't these values that we already endorse? Hopefully this is so, but one of the reasons we can quickly feel like grasshoppers is that our aspirations for honest zeal are easily tempered by compromises in our hearts. If we are feeling inadequate, we may want to make our reports less than fully honest. Sometimes we are tempted to overstate results for the sake of making ourselves look better. At other times we are tempted to understate the truth to make others look bad or to protect ourselves in some way.

When I find myself tempted to put a "spin" on a report, I realize I am on dangerous ground. It is a barometer for me that I am not living from clear, internal convictions but am acting according to the expectations of others. The apostle Paul wrote about these kinds of internal wrestling matches we have with ourselves as the battle between "the spirit and the flesh." In spiritual-formation literature this experience is often referred to as the struggle between the true self and the false self.

In *Coming Home to Your True Self*, Albert Haase writes that one of the key characteristics of the true self is when we live with the conscious and joyful awareness that we are not the center of creation but just one spoke in the giant wheel of what God has created. Such an awareness allows us to then be compassionate, to live with wonder and awe, to be able to focus on the present and to have a passion for peace and justice and love for others. The true self is a self-giving self that freely believes and demonstrates that life is not "all about me."

By way of contrast Haase uses a litany of "p-words" to characterize the false self. Words like *praise, pleasure, position, power, prestige, productivity, perfection* and *possessions*. When we are driven by these needs we lose our spiritual compass by which to align ourselves to God and his purposes, and thus we pursue our own purposes for recognition and leadership control. We are no longer wholehearted; our hearts are divided and we succumb to our innermost fears.

This drives us to the question of how do we become whole-hearted? Is it just being more committed by dint of our will? If this were true, then we push God into the role of helping us carrying out our intentions. We become the creator rather than the created, and God becomes an instrument in our lives rather than the composer of our lives. Obviously this is a dangerous place to be spiritually because it again becomes self-focused, even with the best intentions. Spiritual longings become what John of the Cross called spiritual lusts—wanting spiritual experiences and power for our own benefit and pride, and beyond what God intends for us.

The pathway of wholeheartedness is better described as being able to receive from God what he intends for us. Parker Palmer, in his book *Let Your Life Speak*, tells the Hasidic story of Rabbi Zusya who as an old man said, "In the coming world, they will not ask of me: 'Why were you not Moses?' They will ask of me: 'Why were you not Zusya?' " We live most authentically, freely and wholeheartedly when we live as our true selves in open relationship with our true God.

One other word for wholehearted is *unreserved*, which captures the sense of not only truthfulness but without self-protection. This is hard to do in a culture that is so fearful and is always trying to protect itself. In the financial world we have the Federal Reserve Bank to protect against bank failure. We have insurance to protect against sickness and accident. We have reserve clauses in contracts, and we want reservations for dinner. In other words we want everything to work out perfectly. We don't want to face giants, difficulties or risks.

In our organizational worlds this approach to life manifests itself not only in our business practices but also in our relationships. We do or don't do things so that we won't be blamed. We cover our trails and avoid speaking out for fear of reprisals or embarrassment. We can be afraid to take risks in talking with people out of fear that they will not understand us or respond positively to what we are saying. We want to be like Caleb in seeing the potential of fruit and honey, but we wind up like the other spies that just see the giants.

One of my heroes of wholehearted leadership is John Stott. He has been respectfully referred to as "the Pope of Evangelicalism" because of the tremendous authority and influence he has had in people's lives throughout the world. His pastoral leadership at All Souls Church in London, his powerful expository preaching, his prolific writing and his vision for developing majority-world scholars have all been consistently and extraordinarily successful.

Yet the power of John Stott's authority is not structural but personal. Those who know him well speak of his impeccable integrity of character. His walk with God has been a humble diligence to prayer, Scripture and to loving God and neighbor in all aspects of his life. Without doubt he has been one of the greatest wholehearted Christian leaders in the world in the past half-century.

Ultimately, wholeheartedness reflects a deep faith in God and his calling in our lives. It cannot just be going through the motions. We cannot pretend to be faithful if we just like the comfort of a nice Christian environment or a public Christian identity. Wholeheartedness requires a fullness of commitment that perseveres at the deepest levels of our decision making.

But wholeheartedness is not the same as bravado or foolhardiness. Although it may fit a certain kind of leadership to yell and shout and rally the troops, we see in Caleb someone who is able to quiet the people and speak honestly with his leader, Moses. Caleb did not ignore the giants but wanted to move forward even with their presence. I think this is a good model for leadership. If we pretend that we aren't jealous, fearful or at times succumb to self-pity, we are not being honest with ourselves or others.

Yet neither can these giants immobilize us from taking action. Caleb had a quiet, confident, honest faith in God that reflected a kind of leadership grossly undervalued in our culture of pomp and circumstance. But those were the characteristics that enabled Caleb, and not the other ten spies, to enter the land. In the face of giants, he trusted in God and consequently saw himself as more than a grasshopper.

Perhaps nothing inhibits the external focal point of our leadership ellipse as much as our internal fears. When our inside is self-absorbed with the giants of failure, self-pity, jealousy and ego, we are not able to be courageous or clear in our leadership. We shrink back and don't take risks of faithfulness. But when we have a quiet certainty in God's calling and provision for us, we can enter the promised land of wholehearted leadership.

NINE

As an Organizational Ecologist

The Practice of Attentiveness

Earth is crammed with heaven,
and every common bush is on fire with God;
but only he who sees takes off his shoes;
the rest sit round and pluck blackberries.

ELIZABETH
BARRETT BROWNING

Several years ago I heard an address by Timothy George, the founding dean of Beeson Divinity School, that introduced me to a wonderfully rich concept and word: *ecotone*. He described it as "a word derived from the worlds of biology and ecology. An ecotone is a place where two or more ecosystems come together, . . . like an estuary, where the river flows into the ocean, where the tide meets the current."

But an ecotone is a place of not only tremendous change. It is also an area of great growth potential. Ecotones tend to be places that are fertile with new life brought about by the creative clash of different ecosystems. I find this language of ecology helpful in describing one of the greatest external challenges to any kind of organizational leadership. This is the challenge of keeping various organizational systems and a variety of gifted people in a healthy balance with each other such that growth occurs.

In fact, as I have developed a deeper understanding and practice of leadership over the years, I see that a large part of my job can be described as being an organizational ecologist. I need to understand and guide the diverse and sometimes conflicting elements that are part of any human organization in a way that stimulates both change and a rich relational fecundity. If people are growing as individuals and find satisfaction in their work in concert with the mission of the organization, it is likely that the organization will grow in a healthy way. But if there is always turbulence and conflict, what has the potential for beauty becomes ugly and destructive.

ORGANIZATIONAL TOXICITY

No matter how visionary, well-aligned and committed an organization may be, it can become quickly poisoned by interpersonal conflict. This is especially true if the tension is within the top ranks of leadership. Like contamination in a river that pollutes everything downstream, relational tensions among leaders produce an environment that becomes unhealthy for everybody else.

We see this rather publicly in sports teams. When the coaches and senior players are fighting and yelling at each other, the team is usually in trouble. Players take sides, and the team struggles to compete effectively. However, when a team is winning, players and coaches alike talk about good team chemistry and a good spirit in the locker room.

Yet organizational toxicity and toxic leaders are all too common. In *The Allure of Toxic Leaders*, Jean Lipman-Blumen describes toxic organizations as those with detrimental practices and policies, unreasonable performance goals, "promoting excessive internal competition and creating a culture of blame." Toxic leaders foster and promote such practices due to "enormous egos that blind leaders to the shortcomings of their own character and thus limit their capacity for self-renewal." Toxic leaders create divisiveness rather than unity.

Unfortunately Christian leadership is not always known for its ability to bring people together. Seminaries, parachurch groups and churches can be incubators for divisiveness and spiritual competitiveness. Because Christian leaders have a strong sense of Christian responsibility for serving God and a strong desire to do and be right, we can all too easily justify conflict as the necessary path to truth and righteousness. We persuade ourselves and tell those around us that we are defending the truth, but our protestations can often sound like ego and self-righteousness.

This happens in the marketplace as well but without the spiritual veneer. Departmental leaders vie for prominence with other leaders, and people in their departments follow suit. Marketing fights with production, and sales fights with engineering. Visionaries look down on accountants as bean counters and IT looks at executives as technically challenged or incompetent. Our human tendency is to want others to be like us or at least do their part so we are successful according to our strengths and accountabilities. The heart of prejudice is to think that those who are different from us are inferior in some way, and this attitude erodes trust and creates a toxic environment.

A further complication is that the people we lead also have the same struggles. How can we help them to have better relationships and not live with unresolved tensions? Part of the answer is rooted in who we are. We cannot lead people on paths that we are not willing to walk on, and we cannot do that just by ourselves. We need mentors, pastors, spiritual directors, counselors and close friends who help us see our weaknesses and encourage us to pursue spiritual and emotional health. We need insight, an openness to change and wisdom in how to do so.

But another part of the answer is to practice healthy relationships and to provide a healthy environment for such relationships to develop. When we practice good health habits, we are less likely to become sick. When we foster a healthy relational environment, we are less likely to be a feeding ground for strained relationships and a toxic organizational culture. How do we do this? How can we develop a healthy organizational ecology? Although there are a multitude of things that can be done, the core orienting principle for me is the "practice of attentiveness."

THE PRACTICE OF ATTENTIVENESS

One of the most practical and insightful books for Alice and me in our parenting has been Ross Campbell's *How to Really Love Your Child*. We have taught and recommended it in marriage seminars and have given it to scores of parents with young children. Campbell emphasizes an essential value for parents is to give "focused attention" to their children because children live almost entirely in the present tense. They learn and respond to what is their current experience.

At an adult level author Albert Haase suggests that this characteristic of being in touch with the present tense may be the main reason Jesus uses children as a model for spirituality—that we must become like children in our engagement with our immediate experience to understand the kingdom of God. The eighteenth-century French Jesuit Jean-Pierre de Caussade highlighted the importance of immediate experience when he described it as "the sacrament of the present moment."

The translation of this for leadership is not that we treat others like children but that we become like children ourselves to both understand what God is saying and to meaningfully connect with others in real time. Using a medieval metaphor, de Caussade suggests that we treat a king, when in disguise as a commoner, differently if we recognize him as the king than if we don't. Similarly, when we are aware of the work of God in ordinary circumstances and people, we then pay closer attention to those people and to the promptings of God. When we are able to lead with the conscious awareness of God's continual and immediate presence not only inside of us but also in our external context, we bring spiritual coherence and health to our organizational environment.

When we believe that every conversation is a divine appointment, we are more likely to keep eye contact with people and not look over their shoulders for someone else to talk to. When we are curious about God's activity in someone's life we respond honestly to the person's questions and ask him or her questions rather than just trying to talk through our agenda. We pay attention to others because in doing so we are paying attention to the work of God in their lives. In *The Attentive Life*, Leighton Ford writes, "Paying attention is not a way by which we make something happen but a way to see what is already given to us."

I find such attentiveness difficult. As a leader I want others to pay attention to me, to my vision, to my ideas and needs. Most top-down, command-and-control organizational cultures exhibit this leader-centered orientation as the unofficial if not official way of doing things. This is not all bad; it is often necessary for a good organizational decision making process. But when everyone does what is right in their own eyes, organizational chaos and futility results. An organizational culture becomes unhealthy when most of the focused attention is toward the leader and precious little is given to those who are following.

So I have worked at identifying and practicing various behaviors of attentiveness to guide the use of my time and leadership within the company.

True attentiveness needs to be instinctive and organic—not worked out through a formula. Nevertheless, I've found the following alliterative categories of intentional leadership helpful in training myself to remember how to practice attentiveness to others.

An organizational ecologist

- is involved with people through listening, learning and loving
- invests in people through time, touch and teaching
- inspires people through enunciating vision and providing encouragement

STAYING INVOLVED

The first category of attentive leadership is staying involved with people. This at first seems like a no-brainer. If we are to lead and supervise others, we cannot avoid them. Already most of our working hours are connected with others either through meetings or e-mail or voice contact. But just associating or talking with people is not the same as being involved with them. I remember the humorous but convicting *New Yorker* cartoon of the boss walking around the office saying to people "Good job, whoever you are!"

Most of us have developed the necessary social skills to be able to be friendly in a professional, superficial way, but we often try to avoid meaningful involvement with others because it is too time demanding. When things get messy or too involved, we quickly try to delegate or detach ourselves from the situation because we think we have better and more important things to do.

Once at the beginning of a national conference, I was asked by a senior staff person to meet with him and his wife. I didn't want to do so because I was going to finish my preparations for a presentation I was scheduled to deliver. I suspected it would be a long conversation, and I didn't want to get involved.

But there was something in his request that compelled me to meet with them in a private room. There he tearfully confessed to me that he had committed adultery and was offering his resignation. In doing so he also told me that he had already confessed this destructive sin to God, his wife and to his pastor, and was seeking healing and restoration in all those relationships. He was distraught that not only had he lost the trust of those closest to him, now he was going to lose his job.

As I listened to him, I saw the soul of a strong, gifted man who had been humbled by his own arrogance and weakness. I thought of Jesus' parable of the prodigal son and wondered how I could turn away from him personally or organizationally. I could not just dismiss his betrayal of his leadership position, but neither could I say, "Sorry, it is all over."

So rather than accept his resignation, I embraced him for his honest repentance and organizational integrity. I wept with him and his wife, and I prayed for them both. I then offered him a period of probation for healing and a reestablishment of his commitments to his wife and church, and to his leadership role. His eyes shone with a gratitude I still remember.

I was unprepared for this conversation. I didn't have either emotional or organizational time for it. But Jesus' teaching on the good Samaritan is clearly about being involved with people's needs even when we have other things to do. Yet I struggle with this tension continually. It is not that I don't care but that I am often too preoccupied to be able to care or be involved. So I consciously pray for the prompting of God to help me be attentive and to listen to others.

Listening. Perhaps the greatest expression of attentiveness is listening. It is something we can do so easily, but it takes humility and will power to do it well. As leaders we are used to giving our opinions, giving lectures, giving sermons and giving presentations. Part of our leadership platform is in our ability to speak well and to have something to say. We have to make decisions, we have to cast vision, we have to train and teach others and communicate effectively.

But to be really effective we have to listen even when listening is threatening to our leadership propensity to be in control. When we listen in an active way we are yielding or at least sharing control of the conversation. When we listen for understanding, we are standing under the other person so that the person and his or her story have prominence. Although we may want to give someone our advice or expertise or opinion, what people often want and need the most is simply someone to listen to them. Good listening is good ecology. It helps the systems to function.

Conversely bad listening is toxic to a healthy organizational environment. This often happens in meetings or in personal conversations when one person is speaking and somebody else is so eager to speak that he or she is not listening to what the first person is saying. This person might say, "if I can just piggyback on what you said" and then say something completely unconnected without even being conscious of what was just said. Another common pattern is to say, "I agree with what you are saying" but then disagree because he or she was too busy interrupting to listen to what the other person really said.

Usually this kind of competitive dialogue marginalizes the quieter person or the person without as much positional power. Many women often feel ignored by a one-upmanship kind of male conversation that is characterized more by winning than by listening. Good listening not only takes time but lots of energy. It involves asking good questions and setting aside our own agenda for the sake of the other person. It helps us to know others and it helps them to be known.

My wife, Alice, has a great gift for getting to know people by asking them questions. One of her favorite questions in a social setting is "What would you like me to know about you?" or if she really gets stuck she has been known to ask, "What would you like me to ask you?"!

We can ask similar but more job-related questions like "What do you like most about your job?" or "What do you wish I knew about your work?" Sometimes we don't even have to ask questions because people want to tell us things about what they are doing. One of the greatest compliments we hear as a leader is when someone says to us "thanks for listening." Good listening is not giving answers but giving attention.

Learning. Learning from others is also a form of attentiveness, not only to others but to our own growth. I suspect that most of us are committed to reading, being mentored and learning from those who are experts or have more experience than we do. We go to seminars and are eager to find out what the latest *Harvard Business Review* or trendy leadership book has to say about successful leadership. We want to learn from leadership gurus.

But it is important to learn from those in our organizations and churches that may not have the same academic pedigree, life experience or level of responsibility. If we don't, we can unconsciously become elitist in our learning and miss out on what others have to teach us.

Sometimes I learn from minority people about different ways of interpreting a situation. A Chinese woman and good friend has helped me many times to discern communication dynamics between those with structural power and those without it. A man in our company has tremendous sensitivities to the feelings and reactions of others to decisions when they are being made. Many times I have had to slow down and listen to his counsel and wisdom.

I also try and learn what is important to those who are younger and how they respond to leaders in the boomer generation. In order to be successful in mature organizations many of us have really given our lives not only to our vocational calling but to our specific jobs. When we are consumed with this allegiance, we lose definition between our lives and our jobs. We might be rightfully labeled as those who "live to work," which is so characteristic of but not limited to the boomer generation.

By way of contrast, many younger leaders have a healthier perspective of "working to live," which allows for lives beyond the job and organization. This is a valuable perspective for those of us who have been slaves to our jobs and careers. Learning from those who are different helps us better manage and lead our organizational ecosystem.

Perhaps the key attribute for learning is to be curious. I think of Moses and the burning bush. He had to consciously "turn aside" to see what was happening. If he hadn't been curious enough to notice the burning bush and pay attention to God's presence in it, he would have missed the call of God in his life.

When we are curious about others and learn from them, we not only strengthen our relationship but our whole relational environment. Curiosity is a mindset of humility and a necessary spiritual disposition to be able to listen well and pay attention to others.

Loving. The best definition of *love* is still what is written by Paul in 1 Corinthians 13. Although this chapter is often reserved for marriage ceremonies, it has great application for attentive leadership. Paul says that love is "patient; love is kind; love is not envious or boastful or arrogant or rude. It does not insist on its own way; it is not irritable or resentful; it does not rejoice in wrongdoing, but rejoices in the truth. It bears all things, believes all things, hopes all things, endures all things."

Think how differently our churches, colleges and companies would function if this teaching were a standard operating procedure for leaders. It is not the macho call to arms of "let's take this to the next level," which may be necessary and even inspirational at times but at most other times it can be an imposition of power that is unloving to others who are already overburdened with their work.

Loving others takes time and patience. One of the great inspirational and successful leaders of our time is Jean Vanier, who has established 133 L'Arche communities in 35 countries for people with developmental disabilities. Vanier says that a great message of L'Arche to a frenzied world is "to slow down" and to "embrace God's time." He says that we are afraid of showing weakness and of not succeeding. "Deep inside, we are afraid of not being recognized. So we pretend we are the best. We hide behind power." It takes time to come out of our hiding and to pay attention to others with a loving perspective.

Love, according to Paul, "bears all things" and "believes all things." Such a perspective seems hopelessly naive in a world of selfish ambition. Even Jesus taught that we "should be wise as serpents" in discerning the actions of others. But wise discernment is not the same as a default position of distrusting people and expecting them to earn our trust before we trust them. It is true that some may take advantage of us, but then we can respond with accurate information and take appropriate action.

When we don't live out of a posture of love and trust, our instinct is to immediately blame someone when something goes wrong. That conveniently puts us in a superior position, which may be very misleading in sorting out what really happened. Recently I became aware of a conflict between two of our people that was very unsettling. There was no question in my mind that they were acting in a mutually foolish way.

After I got into the situation though, I discovered that part of their problem was a lack of clarity in job responsibilities that I should have clarified for them previously. It is true that they could have figured it out or asked about the situation, but the loving action was to give them the benefit of the doubt and find out what was causing the conflict.

Sometimes there is also the need for tough love. This happens in spades when we need to discipline someone or fire them for poor performance. But tough love is not just being hardheaded. It requires a love that means that this action will be for the person's best good. I remember Terry Sanford, a former president of Duke

University and a United States Senator, saying that there are three
ways to fire someone. One is to send them a pink slip. The second
is to call them on the phone. The third is to meet with them in
person and then throw up afterward! Needless to say, this is what
he deemed to be the best, because it was the most loving option.

STAYING INVESTED

The second category of leadership attentiveness is investing in
people. When we think of people as mere units of labor or as "giving units" or as worker bees, we demean them and shirk our leadership responsibilities. We need to provide resources and opportunities for them to be healthy and grow. This is not always easy
because sometimes our financial and personnel resources limit
what we can do. But the key is thinking of them and not just us.

Evidently one of the most difficult tasks to do in training a Seeing Eye dog is to get the dog to be able to judge the height of its
master for walking under low objects. The dog knows its own
height, but to judge the height of its master requires lots of practice. Leaders sometimes need to be like Seeing Eye dogs to those
we serve. As we become more aware of where they want to go, we
then can lead them appropriately. To do this well it takes various
measures of time, touch and teaching.

Time. Our most precious commodity is time. What people who
report to us probably most want from us is our time—time to listen
to their challenges and problems, time to help them set good goals
and objectives, time to understand enough of what they are doing
that we can honestly compliment and reward them, and time for
them to know that they are important to us. As leaders we need to
take the time to notice or be attentive to those around us. As I have
discovered in marriage, it is far more valuable for me to compliment
Alice on her new outfit before she tells me that it is new!

There are a variety of ways to give time to people who look to
us for leadership. There is of course the "best practice" of planned

times for review. This kind of basic reporting structure is important because it can be planned and serves as good relational maintenance. Followers need a certain level of predictability in their leaders. Yet sometimes we may find that this kind of meeting may become mechanical or perfunctory. If this is the case, we should discuss what might work better. We don't want to waste people's time or vice versa.

Another proven way to give time is to have an open door policy both literally and figuratively. People who report to us need to know that they can talk with us almost any time they need to within the parameters of a normal schedule of priorities. The openness of availability is a wonderful gift to give to those around us. If they feel like they have to take a ticket, like when waiting at a deli, then they too can feel like sliced meat.

One helpful practice for me to be available is to avoid overplanning my schedule with back-to-back meetings or appointments that don't allow any breathing space or any contingency time for important interruptions. I am encouraged that there is no record of Jesus running anywhere or of being in a hurry. When he was urged to quickly visit Lazarus, he waited two days. But it was because of this waiting that Jesus was then able to perform that greatest of miracles—raising Lazarus from the dead. When we avoid rushing, we are more likely to be able to see God at work in what we do. I never have any problem filling in extra time, and it gives me space for the unexpected needs of others.

The third way we give time to people though is the unexpected time—when we drop in their office, take them to lunch on short notice or find out about their weekend. It is this casual time together that not only is mutually enjoyable but again builds the relationship. If we communicate that we are too busy for people apart from clipped schedules, we create a certain distance that can become a fissure under times of stress. Casual time deepens our investment in others.

Touch. Touch can be both literal and figurative. Although I am not a gregarious person, I find that a genuine handshake, a touch on the arm or an appropriate hug can be a means of telling a person that I care and want to truly be in touch with them. There obviously needs to be high standards and good boundaries so that touch is not in any way manipulative or sexually misleading. Because different people have different levels of comfort with touch, we should never make anyone feel uncomfortable with physical contact. But we are human and natural forms of social and physical connection are important parts of our organizational ecosystem.

The figurative dimension of touch is that we want to add value to people's lives. There used to be a television program titled *Touched by an Angel,* and we talk about being "touched" by something of deep personal meaning. Touching communicates connection and gentleness, and it can even happen in how we look at people.

A friend of mine at church does a lot of international travel. As he goes through the long lines of other travelers, he has established the habit and joyous practice of looking at others and saying to himself with a smile "a child of God." I have no doubt that this humble attitude and his warm smile have touched many people. We too can touch people with our facial expressions when we see them.

Perhaps the most significant kind of touch we give, though, is our emotional touch. This is when we are fully engaged and responsive to what others are feeling. If they are feeling hurt, frustrated or misunderstood, they are not likely to be satisfied with mere answers or solutions to their problems. Similarly if they are excited about success, they want us to be able to share in their joy.

Some of us are more emotionally attuned and are able to do this somewhat naturally. But many times, we are so busy or consumed with our own problems that we don't have the emotional energy to respond effectively to the emotions of others. We are like parents of teenagers that get blind-sided with their children's deep problems when they thought everything was going well. We need an emotional intelligence that takes time and sensitivity to others. We also need to be in touch with our own feelings as well.

Teach. John W. Alexander was a natural educator. He was professor and chair of the geography department at the University of Wisconsin and then became president of InterVarsity for sixteen years. John loved to invest in young people and was always creating new training programs to do this. At the heart of his training philosophy was the acronym TDOEE, which stands for teach, demonstrate, observe, evaluate and encourage. It was not rocket science but was a very helpful framework for how best to invest in others, and it began with teaching.

In today's working environment, many do not look to their leaders for instruction. They learn in different ways and from different people, and too much overt and unrequested teaching from a leader can be counterproductive. People like to peel their own learning banana.

But in our role as leaders we likely know or have experienced more than others that can be of great benefit to them. Sometimes in an egalitarian society we may be shy about sharing ourselves or information that would enable others to grow. Because we don't want the image of being a "know it all," we may not give to others what might be valuable to them. Also because knowledge is power we may intentionally withhold information for fear that we might become obsolete.

Yet we do have a leadership obligation to teach what we have learned for the sake of others. At the center of the apostle Paul's mission was a commitment to teaching everyone. How do we do this without being "teachy"? The key is in the attitude that comes from within us. If we are teaching others to impress them, we may well be marginalized in our effectiveness. Followers can intuitively and easily discern our intentions. However, when we teach others in the spirit of offering ourselves to them, then we are being attentive to their needs and investing in them.

INSPIRING OTHERS

The third category of being an organizational ecologist is inspiring others by enunciating vision and empowering or encouraging them to use their gifts to their fullest. These are common leadership traits but they are worth mentioning in the context of organizational ecology because we must candidly recognize that sometimes people resist being inspired. When Joseph Strauss composed the "Music of the Spheres" to draw people's attention to God's creation, people rejected it. They didn't want to be reminded of the heavenlies while at a ball!

Sometimes we may try to inspire people and they resist because of their own spiritual battles. The danger comes when we try to inspire them through our self-conscious leadership energy. It is far better to not think of us but of them and their need to flourish in our organizational ecotone. Then we are better able to inspire and enunciate vision.

Enunciating vision. A standard practice for most institutions, ministries and churches is enunciating vision and values. We go through long processes and meetings to produce statements that everybody agrees to—or at least everybody that was working on the process! But the statements are not the most important thing, talking about them is. One of our most crucial roles as leaders is to talk about what is important to us and to our leadership. We need to continually communicate what we are doing, why we are doing it and where we are going.

One thing I do is to meet individually with everyone who joins our company to go over our purpose and values. The reason for this is both to build a relational contact with everyone and to say that these values are important to me and to InterVarsity Press. We use our values to recruit people, and we send our values statement to authors so they have a missional context that goes beyond a contract for working with us. We also refer to our purpose and values regularly in our internal meetings for strategy and review. I've included them in an appendix for your interest.

Encouragement. Everybody needs personal encouragement, especially encouragement to be successful in their jobs. When I worked for Ford Motor Company in my college days, I was in charge of a project change that had major quality-control ramifications. At the end of the project I received a piece of notepaper from Harry Gladding, who was the head of quality control for the entire plant I was working in. On this note were the simple words "very nicely done." The fact that I still remember (and have) his written pat on the back from a senior leader is evidence of how powerful even a few words of encouragement can be.

Like yawning, encouragement is infectious. When encouraged, we are more likely to encourage others. Our receptionist says that her job description is to be "in charge of first impressions," and she fulfills her job in such positive ways by being an encouragement to everyone who walks through our door. Consequently, people like to visit InterVarsity Press just to see Audrey.

We also encourage and empower people in a variety of ways, from giving them flexible hours, personalized projects and the opportunity to grow through taking initiative and even making mistakes. One of the easiest and best ways to empower others is through open, easy access to information decision-making processes. If people feel that they know what is going on and are able to contribute to meaningful decisions, they are even more empowered in their own particular job responsibilities.

FOSTERING A HEALTHY CLIMATE

Being an organizational ecologist is not simple or easy. In any structure there are systems and people who have great potential to do harm to one another. It is not "natural" for people from a vari-

ety of backgrounds to spend 50 percent of their waking hours
working together without conflict or some form of dysfunctional
behavior. Our sinful, selfish propensities exacerbate these points
of conflict as we strive for any kind of personal advantage. Without intentional leadership that provides a healthy climate for personal growth and collective accomplishment, our work lives de-
generate into disappointment and drudgery. But when we practice
attentiveness in a way that is rooted to our integrity and calling as
leaders, we are able to be effective organizational ecologists.

TEN

As a Grateful Creature

The Practice of Clarity

Gratitude follows grace like thunder lightening.

KARL BARTH

I first met Max De Pree at a board meeting. In his day job, Max was CEO of the highly esteemed Herman Miller office furniture company. But on this occasion Max was using his leadership gifts to chair the board of Fuller Theological Seminary in Pasadena, California. I was there as an invited guest to talk with the Fuller board about undergraduate college students, who formed a large pool of potential students for the seminary.

I don't remember what I said, but I do remember what people said about Max. They spoke of his wisdom and his care for people and his ability to lead successfully in a very competitive business. Although I only had the chance that day to say hello, I made a mental note to try to find another opportunity to be with Max and learn from him.

That opportunity came in the following year when I attended a weeklong leadership seminar for those like myself who had job responsibilities in the area of human resources. The seminar was co-led by Max and a distinguished ethics professor at Fuller,

Lewis Smedes. This was a stimulating time about the ways people should be treated in our organizations. Lew raised various ethical issues of fairness and honesty while Max talked about the practical challenges and opportunities of applying these principles in business situations.

At first the issues and the answers seemed rather basic. Of course, Christian leaders should be honest, ethical and caring about those we lead. There was no disagreement on what seemed like obvious Christian virtues. We all wanted to do what was right.

But as we got deeper into the guts of our job responsibilities, I became more aware that just knowing and wanting to do good was not the same as being able to fulfill those intentions. I realized how often in leadership I felt like the apostle Paul, who confessed that he was not able to do what he wanted to do. At one point he publicly castigated himself with the angry denunciation, "Wretched man that I am!" (Rom 7:24). I had not used those words as such, but I had felt similar feelings of deep frustration and regret over my failings in leadership.

So as I recognized my need for help, I listened more carefully to Max and Lew and the others in the seminar. What stood out the most in all of our discussions was the theme of being thankful in leadership and for those we lead. We talked about leaders living from a spirit of abundance that enriches people rather than from a spirit of scarcity that pits people against each other.

I connected this with Paul's subsequent testimony in Romans 8 that an answer to my experience of inadequacy was thanking God and welcoming others in the same way I had been welcomed by Jesus. Paul was not being simplistic but doxological in his attitudes and orientation.

This put into context Max's profound and succinct definition of leadership as "defining reality and saying thank you." Of all the books I have read and the seminars I have attended on leadership, this has been the most spiritually and practically helpful perspective on leadership.

Consequently, in this last chapter I want to share some specific ways of how this perspective of clarity and gratitude has helped give shape to my leadership ellipse, bringing together my outer work life and my inner spiritual life. It is not a magic formula that should be slavishly copied but rather a testimony of how God is answering my prayer for a life of internal and external integrity.

BEING A CREATURE

Although it may seem unflattering at first, I use the term *creature* in this chapter's title as far more than a unifying literary device for this book. I use it to remember that I am created by God and that my life is most satisfying and congruent when I live in that reality. I need the reminder that I am not God and he is.

Knowing our creaturely limitations is also a fundamental but perhaps elusive conviction for us to keep at the forefront of our thoughts and actions. When we have power and authority over people it is all too easy to start believing that therefore we are always right. This is especially true when others flatter us or in extreme situations even idolize us as leaders.

At the end of the Revelation to St. John, an angel reveals dramatic visions of the future to the apostle. The aged saint responds to the angel by falling down to worship at the angel's feet. But the angel said, "You must not do that! I am a fellow servant [creature] with you. . . . Worship God!" (Rev 22:9). Like John we need that exhortation to only worship God, and like the angel we need that instinctual reaction to deflect the desires of others to put us on a pedestal. We lead others best when we fully recognize that we are all fellow creatures.

But just as we should not idolize others or allow others to idolize ourselves, neither should we idolize our gifts—even the gift of leadership. This tragically happened with Gideon in ancient Israel. Although he started out as a reluctant leader, he became quite successful as a military hero. As a visible recognition of his accomplishments, he requested a beautiful jeweled vestment to be made, which was called an ephod. But the people of Israel "prostituted themselves to it there, and it became a snare to Gideon and to his family" (Judg 8:27). The ephod became Gideon's burden and led to his leadership decline.

A helpful antidote to pride is accepting and even embracing our limitations. I know of a successful pastor who doesn't do counseling because he discovered that even after he told people the right answers they still needed help the following week! He realized that he is a teacher that can articulate truth but that he doesn't have the pastoral gifts to walk along with people as they gradually live out those truths. Similarly, we can't do it all. We have limits. We are all fellow servants and creatures.

I had a dramatic creaturely experience when I was hiking in Denali State Park in Alaska. I was disappointed that I had not yet seen any major wildlife up close when I was startled by a cow moose eating some leaves at the edge of the trail less than ten feet in front of me. After my initial shock of being confronted by such a large animal, I quickly checked to see if she had any calves with her, which would have made her much more dangerous.

Fortunately she was alone and seemed far more interested in the trees she was nibbling than in me. However, I could not get past her and wound up watching her eat for nearly ten minutes. As my heart rate slowed I was entranced to observe her just being a moose. She was doing what moose do when they are hungry. She was fulfilling her created purpose and giving tribute to her Maker just in her existence. One of the reasons I love to observe animals in the wild is that they are not full of pretense but are living their natural lives. I am taught by their unadorned creatureliness.

GRATITUDE

However, we are more than just creatures of instinct. We have been created in God's image to live in relationship with him and all of his creation. This involves caring for the environment and for one another. We have not been created in isolation for the sake of our own glory. Rather we have been created for God's glory.

But in a glorious circular reality we are most glorified when we are grateful to God and give him glory for his creation. C. S. Lewis wrote in his monograph *The Weight of Glory* that the most creaturely of pleasures is "the specific pleasure of the inferior." He goes on to say that "When human souls have become as perfect in voluntary obedience as the inanimate creation is in its lifeless obedience, then they will put on its glory, or rather the greater glory of which nature is only the first sketch."

I experienced a bit of this truth when I was once asked to lead an outdoor Vespers service on a sandy shore in the Upper Peninsula of Michigan. My back was to the water and to a brilliant sunset as I faced about fifty recent college graduates who had come to this time of worship. It was an idyllic setting.

As I glanced up from the liturgy, I thought I was missing out on the beauty of the sunset and was tempted to turn around and watch it. Everyone was far more captivated by it than the order of service. But then I noticed that the sunset was being reflected on the glowing faces of those in the group. For a moment, I realized that the greater beauty that evening was not in the aura of colors embedded in cloud particles behind me but in the faces of the people in front of me, who were worshiping God. Lewis goes on to say in *The Weight of Glory*, "there are no ordinary people" and "next to the Blessed Sacrament itself, your neighbor is the holiest object presented to your senses."

Because our neighbors and coworkers are holy in the sense of being set apart by God in creation, we have the privilege of not only living with them but being grateful for them—or in Max De Pree's

words, "saying thank you." This may not sound difficult, and technically it isn't. Gratitude doesn't take much physical energy or elab-
orate resources. Gratitude in fact is a marvelous human emotion. It
is energizing. It is satisfying. It enriches the soul and those that are
touched by it. Gratitude is not possessive but builds up and it
reaches out. Gratitude cannot be purchased or mimicked or stored.
It can't be achieved or accomplished, because it is not something
that is ever finished or that can be checked off.

Rather, gratitude is the involuntary response of the heart to all
aspects of life and ultimately to God. It is not based primarily on
circumstances. Some of the most grateful people in the world are
the poorest, while many that are rich often are characterized by
their lack of gratitude as they seek to acquire more money or fame.
If this is the case, what then makes us grateful, or how can we be
more grateful people?

One way is to practice the posture of being able to receive rather
than developing our ability to get. Getting or acquiring is something we do that is very self-focused. It feeds our pride. Receiving
however is linked to what others have done or given to us and is
closely linked to humility. To truly receive from others means that
we recognize the intrinsic value of others and what they are giving
to us. This conscious or even unconscious realization is the fertile
soil from which gratitude grows. We can try to force an attitude of
gratitude by saying all of the right things, but if the soil of humility
is not there our gratitude appears gratuitous, superficial or phony.

Another and more difficult dimension of receiving is when
there are serious problems involved. We may instinctively react to
such situations very negatively and even harshly demanding that
the problem be fixed or people be rashly blamed. But Max De Pree
quotes David Hubbard as saying, "leaders don't inflict pain, they
bear pain." This is a practical application of the spiritual reflection
of Parker Palmer: "the way of the cross is the way of absorbing
pain and not passing it on." We may not think we are being grate-

ful when we absorb pain, but it is one of the deepest expressions of gratitude we can offer.

Although it is difficult, I do believe we can practice habits of gratitude. One such habit for me is expressing thanksgiving to God in conscious prayer for all of the individuals that I relate to on a daily basis—my peers, my supervisor, those who report to me and those I do business with. This may not sound very hard, but it is for me because I almost automatically analyze the faults and weaknesses in others. This makes me feel better by comparison and can also give me competitive advantage in jockeying for power or control. Such an unbridled approach to people quenches a spirit of thanksgiving or gratitude for them, even when I want to have it. I feel that I am either being dishonest or spiritually manipulative.

But when I privately pray for people with thanksgiving for who they are, their gifts and their contributions to my life, I am much more likely to be grateful for them in public—even knowing their shortcomings. I experience the gracious work of God's Spirit in gradually transforming my attitudes toward others through prayer.

Gratitude is indeed a gift to others. It communicates that they are valuable and builds trust. When we are grateful and we create a climate of gratitude in our work environment, we enjoy each other more and are inspired to work together better. Conversely when we are highly critical, our relational energy is drained and we live in tension rather than freedom.

The heart of being a grateful creature is found in our relationship with our Creator. As we embrace the theological and practical reality that we and everyone else has been created in the image of God, we can live as grateful creatures in concert with our Creator. As we fully accept our humanity with all of its limitations and sinfulness, we can be profoundly grateful to God for saving us from our sins through the death of Jesus. As we work with others, we can lead them by defining reality and saying thank you.

THE PRACTICE OF CLARITY

At first clarity may seem like a strange practice to link with gratitude. Gratitude can be spontaneous and exuberant, but clarity
seems limiting and even calculating. Clarity, though, is essential
for gratitude to be fully expressed, and they are wonderful companions in the workplace. When we see clearly why we are doing
something, it is much easier to be excited about it. When we define reality and help others see clearly what they are doing, we
create a synergy of understanding and partnership.

This is especially true for those in younger generations who
have lower tolerances for ambiguity and uncertainty. They want to
know what is expected of them and how they might receive recognition and gratitude for their work. It is why good, clear job and
role expectations are so desired and necessary. In a world of unlimited possibilities, clarity gives meaning and direction.

Clarity is also a form of naming, and naming is a biblical practice. In the Garden, Adam's first act of work was to name the animals. When Moses got exhausted in leadership, God taught him
to delegate and to name his limitations. Jesus called and named
the disciples. In a future day, the name of Jesus, not a generic
spirituality, will cause all knees to bow. The New Testament tells
us that every family on earth is named because every family is
important.

Even when things are difficult, naming provides freedom.
When we are sick, we find solace when the illness is named. Then
we know how to live with it. I met with a student once who was
unconsciously obnoxious in his behavior. I took the liberty to ask
him if he knew why people were avoiding him. He hesitantly but
genuinely wanted to know, so I told him the behaviors that were
causing the problems. Remarkably he listened and changed because he now had a clear understanding of what was wrong. Defining reality was a gift to him.

It is also tremendously important to define and clarify our own leadership roles and motivations. A good framework for this is the shepherd image because it is the most familiar and frequent metaphor for leadership in the Bible. We are familiar with the words of Psalm 23, "The LORD is my shepherd," and also know that Jesus refers to himself as "the good shepherd." So it is not a surprise that other biblical writers use this image as well.

The apostle Peter wrote two letters to some early Christians who were facing persecution and had to function as a church with far more organizational challenges than our most difficult market conditions. They were spread out, they were being challenged intellectually about their faith, they had to contend with false prophets, and they were suffering for what they believed to be right. In this context Peter writes to the leaders of these dispersed churches and exhorts them, "Be shepherds of God's flock that is under your care, watching over them—not because you must, but because you are willing, as God wants you to be; not pursuing dishonest gain, but eager to serve, not lording it over those entrusted to you, but being examples to the flock" (1 Peter 5:2-3 TNIV).

Several important leadership values are immediately evident. First there is the clarity of intentionality that undercuts the belief that leadership is just finding out what people want. Leadership that is based solely on opinion polls and the desire to be popular is very common in a democratic society. Although it is essential to know what people think and desire, we abdicate our leadership by not adding value and giving shape to their opinions. Tending the flock is not a passive leadership posture.

The second leadership value that Peter lays out is related to leadership motivation. He strongly asserts that leadership should not be out of compulsion, greed or the need for power. Rather, leadership should emanate from a spirit of willingness, eagerness and personal integrity. We need to lead by example. Although this seems rather straightforward, it is neither automatic nor easy because of what is happening inside of us. It's the peacock's prayer all over again—our inside and outside are not working together in harmony. But pursuing clear, selfless motives enables us to lead with integrity of character.

SEEK SPIRITUAL DIRECTION

A classic form for gaining clarity and spiritual discernment in our lives is to pursue spiritual direction with a gifted spiritual director. This has long been a practice within the Catholic Church, but recently it has become more available and appreciated in many Protestant circles as well. Spiritual direction is so highly regarded because we all have spiritual blind spots and are unable to clearly see our weaknesses. We need the help of others to gently help us be aware of what hinders us in our spiritual growth.

My wife is a spiritual director and sometimes describes her role as being a chiropractor of the soul. She chose this image after going to a chiropractor for lower back pain. As he moved up and down her spine, he asked, "Does that hurt?" It turned out that often the source of the pain was not where it presented itself. Similarly, the gentle questions of a spiritual director often reveal unconscious places of emotional or spiritual pain, places that need the healing "balm of Gilead."

I too go to a spiritual director and find that my time with him is a valuable spiritual exercise. It not only makes me face my limitations but also helps me receive God's grace in greater ways. Once I went when I was very weary in my work and felt detached from God. Basically, I wanted a pat on the back for all that I was doing.

What I received though was a reminder that Jesus came to earth and lived a very earthly life of weariness and rejection. My spiritual director enabled me to see my leadership as more than being too busy but a sharing of Christ's sufferings. This wasn't the psychological boost I was hoping for, but it was a profound spiritual message that provided far deeper comfort for me.

Not everyone can have or may even want a spiritual director as such. However, I believe it is important that all leaders have a person or people who function as more than an accountability group and who give us genuine feedback on our spiritual journey. Accountability groups tend to focus more on external behaviors, which is valuable, but we also need help to be more in touch with God.

In *Seeking God Together,* my wife Alice writes about group spiritual direction as "a place where individuals can experience what it means to be listened to and loved by others, so that they can learn to listen more attentively to God in their daily lives and be used by God to spread God's grace and love throughout the world." Whether we are part of a spiritual direction group, a covenant group or a Bible study group, we will gain necessary clarity and direction in our spiritual lives when the agenda is shaped to help each other listen to God and to each other.

RULE OF LIFE

Another good way of practicing clarity is through a rule of life, which is best known from the Benedictine practice developed in the sixth century. Originally it was very extensive and detailed every aspect of the day and night. If you visit a Benedictine monastery you will likely find a modern and simplified version of it available. You will also see it practiced by those who live there. Benedict created his rule to bring together a collection of monks and help shape them into a meaningful spiritual community. Since then other communities have adopted or adapted Benedict's rule.

There are also many descriptions of a rule of life. In *Sacred Rhythms*, Ruth Haley Barton describes a rule of life as a way of "cultivating rhythms for spiritual transformation." Anne Elizabeth McLoughlin suggests that a rule of life includes four basic elements—prayer, community, work and rest. These elements form walls that can protect us from dissipating our lives. For instance, prayer is a wall that keeps us in a right relationship with

God, community keeps us in a right relationship with others of faith, and rest keeps us in a right relationship with ourselves.

But what is most intriguing and insightful to me about a rule of life is the emphasis on work as an element of life that best allows us to share in God's creative activity in the world. Benedict did not idolize work as the only place to find our identity and value. But neither did he dismiss it or diminish it as a form of evil that we have to endure in order to be able to indulge in more spiritual or enjoyable parts of life. Rather he recognized that meaningful work is to be part of a healthy human experience.

There is dignity to work that reflects part of the character of God. God worked in creating the world and continues to work in redeeming the world. When we work we share in God's intentions and his very nature. In *Culture Making*, Andy Crouch calls Christians to embrace both the calling and the opportunities to be actively involved in making and shaping all aspects of culture for the glory of God. This is beyond what Benedict had in mind, but they both share this spirit of work as a way of worshiping God rather than our contemporary tendency to worship work instead.

If you have never heard of a rule of life, it may not sound like the most appealing way to strengthen your leadership. Yet most of us seek a comprehensive and disciplined framework for how we live. Even those of us who may be extremely gifted and charismatic in our leadership will crash and burn if we don't recognize our limitations and discipline ourselves accordingly.

But typically when leaders feel a need to improve, we read another leadership book or go to a leadership seminar. We make New Year's resolutions. We watch what we eat. We go to the gym. We decide to try having a devotional time, again. At work, we try to structure our time better. It seems that trying to stay competent in our leadership roles demands that we continually reorganize ourself and others. There is always the hope that by restructuring what we are doing, we will solve our problems and have greater success.

Yet our experience tells us that even if we feel an immediate lift with our new patterns of dedication, old patterns return and we feel stuck once again. Or we may be making some good changes but those around us aren't. Often a real part of our leadership frustration is that we can't control how everyone else is going to respond to our initiatives.

Sometimes I think of the joke about the retiring executive who leaves three envelopes in his desk for his successor to open when she gets in a crisis. After only a few months the new leader feels stuck and opens the first envelope and the note says "Reorganize." This seems like sage advice, which she heeds and subsequently experiences new energy and success in her job.

However a year or two later, the company was struggling again, so she opened the second envelope which too says "Reorganize." Again she takes this advice and does a major overhaul among all those who report to her, and again things lurch forward. Pleased with her wise actions, she leads her company with confidence—until she again feels stuck. She is reluctant to open the last envelope, suspecting she knows what it says. But she opens it and is surprised to read "Prepare three envelopes."

Sometimes reorganization works, and as leaders we can't afford to be stuck or let others get stuck in their jobs. But often the reasons for our "stuckness" are more internal than external. Because our lives are not coherent, our interior life is not well connected with our exterior responsibilities and we radiate this dissonance. The dissonance may also be a reflection of issues from our family of origin or from other previous relationships. We can't change our past, but neither do we have to be trapped by it.

A rule of life is different from good leadership principles or effective time-management habits because it is the spiritual integration of our lives. It takes our aspirations and connects them with God's desires for our lives. It articulates our hopes and guides us in our decisions. Ultimately it may be the most practical advice I can give to develop the practice of clarity.

DEVELOPING PERSONAL RULE OF LIFE

I conclude this chapter by sharing with you what is currently my own rule of life. I confess I am both reluctant and embarrassed to do so. Putting something in writing for public consumption prompts feelings of great inadequacy. I wish that my rule were more spiritually incisive or offered profound new leadership directions. It is neither like the motivational *Seven Habits of a Highly Effective Executive* by Stephen Covey nor the mystical *Seven Storey Mountain* by Thomas Merton. However, it is mine, written in the context of my life before God and others.

Consequently, I share it with you with three caveats. First, this rule of life did not happen overnight but has grown and changed over the years. As you will readily see, much of what I have written in this book flows in and out of my rule. So as I learn more about myself and how I want to live in harmony with who I am and God's calling, I feel free to add, delete or otherwise change what I have written and intend to practice in my life. A rule of life is best seen as a servant, not a master.

Second, I do not always follow my rule. Sometimes this is circumstantial. Because I travel a great deal and often have to adjust my schedule and priorities to the needs of others, I am not always able to do what I want to do. Sometimes I am just too tired, and sometimes I just don't want to be disciplined. But it is easier to live with exceptions than to live in a vacuum. The goal is not to have a perfect rule or even to follow one perfectly. The goal is following Jesus in our lives and our leadership.

Third, I think everyone benefits from a rule of life when it is carved out of his or her own life and relationship with God. Because we are uniquely created and called, the disciplines that are needed to further shape our lives in accordance with God's good purposes will vary with each of us. What is best for me may not fit you. In sharing these personal intentions I do not suggest you should have the same practices. I hope that if you have never practiced a rule of life before, maybe this example will help you get started. So feel free to use what I list below as a template or as a stimulus to pursue a rule of life for your own use.

Not every leader has or needs a written rule of life to be an effective Christian leader. However, I am convinced that every leader that wants to have a spiritually coherent life needs to gratefully and intentionally pursue a spiritually disciplined life. Using the nautical metaphor of Isaiah 33:23, we don't want the rigging of our lives to hang loose. Rather we need the basic spiritual framework of our lives to sustain us in the midst of the storms and heavy winds of life.

My rule of life is built in response to the Great Commandments. They touch all aspects of my life and leadership calling. It is framed by my desires, which I pray to be translated into actions.

I desire to cultivate and order the affections of my heart by having

- a quiet heart that is refreshed by weekly sabbath rest
- a pruned heart that is cleansed daily by God's forgiveness
- a dancing heart that is attentive to serving others

I desire to nurture the inclinations of my soul by having

- a daily devotional time of prayer and Bible study
- a daily filling and dependence on the Holy Spirit
- a daily spiritual discernment for my day's activities

I desire to strengthen the disciplines of my mind by having

- a renewed mind that is reading and reflecting on biblical truth
- a spiritual mind that is honoring rather than dishonoring others

- a prepared mind that is engaged with my responsibilities

I desire to practice the habits of my strength by

- sufficient sleep of seven hours a night
- a healthy diet
- vigorous exercise three times per week
- avoidance of all forms of pornography
- limited times of watching television

I desire to be faithful to my family by

- being attentive to Alice in all aspects of our life together
- loving and caring for our children and grandchildren
- staying in good communication with our extended family

I desire to be committed to my local church and Christian community by

- active participation in the corporate life of our church
- commitment to our covenant group
- tithing and supporting the ministry of our church and missionaries
- being involved with the issues and acts of justice and compassion in the world

I desire to be a good steward of my vocational calling by leading with

- a wholehearted commitment to God's kingdom
- a visionary focus for my leadership responsibilities
- an active involvement with others as an organizational ecologist
- a dedication to encouraging and investing in others
- gratitude and clarity

The final part of my rule is reciting a prayer that to the best of my current understanding summarizes the desires and inclinations of my heart and mind. I suspect it too will change in the future, but I offer it to you as my testimony of God's grace and leading in my life.

Lord, grant me a quiet, contented soul that is neither distraught with internal regrets nor frenzied by external circumstances or immobilized by fears of loss, but rather finds its peace and satisfaction in you.

Please prune my life from temporal attachments and entanglements so that I may love you with all of my heart, soul, mind and strength, and love my neighbor as myself.

I pray that you would also create in me a humble mind to learn from others and to understand, obey and delight in your Word.

And grant me a dancing heart of joy that is attentive to others and engages the world around me with you and your kingdom.

Fill and direct me with your Holy Spirit that I may wholeheartedly lead and serve others with beauty, wisdom, gratitude and purpose as an instrument of your grace and to the glory of your name.

Amen.

Epilogue

If I had to choose one word that captures the essence of
Christian character it would be integrity. To have integrity is to be whole,
in the sense that all of your parts—all of the elements that make you up—
are properly in place and working together in a harmonious fashion.

RICHARD MOUW

I began this book by quoting the poetic prayer of a peacock that bemoaned the dissonance between its inner and outer lives. It felt beautiful on the outside yet ugly on the inside. But the peacock also prayed for intrapersonal reconciliation and harmony to develop so that there would be integrity in all aspects of its life.

I have identified with both parts of that prayer, especially with respect to my leadership calling. In the language of the leadership ellipse, I want both the focal point of my internal spiritual life to compliment and shape the focal point of my external leadership.

This has been a prayer of longing and hope for me because it prompts me to pursue spiritual formation in a way that brings wholeness to both my private and public life. I am no longer content to live with self-centered pious practices or self-centered external measures of success. Instead I desire to have an internal vibrancy of soul that bears witness to God's grace in me and through me in the world.

In the first chapter I described the opening class at Regent College that was so discouraging to me. I want to conclude by finishing that part of my story.

On the last day of class we were asked to do another drawing, but this time the assignment was to picture what we had learned and experienced in class. I again drew a tree, but instead of a scraggly tree that barely showed signs of life, this time I drew a tree in full spring blossom. The title I put at the bottom of this picture was not a cry of desperation but a statement of hope from the psalms, "Let all the trees of the forest sing for joy" (Ps 96:12 TNIV).

Christian hope is different from optimism or seeing life as a glass that is half full. Optimism can be a valuable trait in leadership, but it also can be misleading when it is based merely on a style of temperament or when it denies reality. True hope is not a denial but an affirmation in the God of hope, who chooses to work through us for the sake of his glory. It is this kind of genuine hope that allows us to lead with joy.

May the God of hope and joy encourage and strengthen all of us to pursue and practice the kind of spiritual integrity in our lives that will shape our leadership for the sake of God's kingdom, here on earth as it is in heaven.

Appendix

InterVarsity Press Purpose and Values Statement

Our Purpose

As an extension of InterVarsity Christian Fellowship/USA, Inter-Varsity Press serves those in the university, the church and the world by publishing resources that equip and encourage people to follow Jesus as Savior and Lord in all of life.

Our Values

Love for God, God's Word, God's People and God's Purposes in the World

Our identity is rooted in our affections for God, whom we seek to worship in spirit and in truth. We wholeheartedly affirm the authority and teachings of the Bible as foundational for our lives and for our publishing decisions. We love the church, respect and feed on its rich heritage, and desire to serve it with grace and truth. We seek to influence, engage and shape the university world and our contemporary culture for the sake of Jesus Christ and his kingdom in the world.

Thoughtful Integration of Life

We value ideas and their careful expression. We love the life of the mind and want to "take captive every thought and make it obedient to Jesus Christ." We aim for integration of the whole person—our hearts tutored by truth, our minds shaped by godly affections, our bodies and souls surrendered with joy to God's good purposes.

Dignity of People and Relationships

We value all people as created in the image of God. We celebrate each person's contribution of gender, ethnicity, church heritage and personality. We practice a collegial approach to our work that entrusts others with meaningful opportunities and responsibilities. We value open and honest relationships. We care about authors, customers, students, campus staff, vendors and each other as people we can serve with joy, attentiveness and trustworthy business transactions. We love to work and to have fun!

Beauty and Stewardship in Our Work

We value excellence, eloquence, creativity, skill and innovation. We desire to produce, package and distribute books and other resources in ways that reflect the glory of God. We like working in an environment that is clean and attractive, and exhibits the beauty of God's peace. We also value financial integrity and faithful accounting of our business activities. We strive to be responsible and wise in using our resources of time, energy and money.

FOR CONTEMPLATION
AND ACTION

CHAPTER 1: A WEANED SOUL

1. What most helps you to have a quiet heart? How can you best preserve that in your life?

2. How do you honor the sabbath? How would you like to honor the sabbath?

3. Practice taking some time each day away from electronic noise and availability.

CHAPTER 2: A GROWING STRENGTH

1. What actions and attitudes habitually undercut your relationship with God and others?

2. What disordered affections are in your life? Pray for God's help to let go of them.

3. Choose to forgive others when they offend you. Pray to receive God's forgiveness.

CHAPTER 3: A RENEWED MIND

1. Identify and pray against the thought patterns that draw you away from God.

2. Reflect on Philippians 4:8 and the things in your life that are true, honorable, just.

3. Consider starting or joining a book group.

CHAPTER 4: A DANCING HEART

1. Pursue some form of art, music or literature that allows your heart to dance.

2. When you pray for your day, anticipate being "a present" to others.

3. Choose a social concern ministry outside of your vocation that helps you serve others.

CHAPTER 5: IN A FRENZIED WORLD

1. Slowly pray the Lord's Prayer and listen to the Spirit's promptings within you.

2. What would it be like to "ruthlessly eliminate hurry" in your life?

3. Do something in your leadership to make life less frenzied for those you lead.

CHAPTER 6: IN A LONELY WORLD

1. Reflect for an extended period of time on what it means for you to belong to God.

2. How can you better belong in the world without the world belonging in you?

3. What can you do in your leadership to strengthen belonging among those you lead?

CHAPTER 7: IN A FRAGMENTED WORLD

1. Pray for shalom (peace) in the relationships that give you the most problems.

2. How might you strengthen your multiethnic and gender relationships?

3. Lead your team in committing to practicing reconciliation among those in conflict.

CHAPTER 8: AS MORE THAN A GRASSHOPPER

1. What most quickly precipitates self-pity within you? Practice not blaming others.

2. What are the giants in your life that make you feel small in the eyes of others?

3. Pray for a wholehearted vision for yourself and your team.

CHAPTER 9: AS AN ORGANIZATIONAL ECOLOGIST

1. Identify the healthy and unhealthy ecosystems in your work environment.

2. How would you like to be more involved with those you lead?

3. How would you like to invest more in those you lead?

CHAPTER 10: AS A GRATEFUL CREATURE

1. Pray for opportunities to gratefully receive from others.

2. Develop a conscious practice of genuinely and immediately thanking people.

3. Develop a rule of life that shapes your external leadership by who you are internally.

RECOMMENDED READING

Barton, Ruth Haley. *Strengthening the Soul of Your Leadership.* Downers Grove, Ill.: InterVarsity Press, 2008.

Bass, Dorothy C. *Receiving the Day.* San Francisco: Jossey-Bass, 2000.

Becket, John D. *Loving Monday.* Downers Grove, Ill.: InterVarsity Press, 2006.

Beebe, Gayle D., and Richard J. Foster. *Longing for God.* Downers Grove, Ill.: InterVarsity Press, 2009.

Benner, David G. *The Gift of Being Yourself.* Downers Grove, Ill.: InterVarsity Press, 2004.

Calhoun, Adele Ahlberg. *Spiritual Disciplines Handbook.* Downers Grove, Ill.: InterVarsity Press, 2005

Charry, Ellen T. *By the Renewing of Your Minds.* New York: Oxford University Press, 1999.

Dawn, Marva. *Keeping the Sabbath Wholly.* Grand Rapids: Eerdmans, 1989.

De Pree, Max. *Leadership Is an Art.* East Lansing: Michigan State University Press, 1987.

Ford, Leighton. *The Attentive Life.* Downers Grove, Ill.: InterVarsity Press, 2008.

Fryling, Alice. *Too Busy?* Downers Grove, Ill.: InterVarsity Press, 2002.

Gardner, John W. *Self-Renewal.* New York: Harper & Row, 1964.

Griffin, Emilie. *The Reflective Executive.* New York: Crossroad, 1993.

Haase, Albert. *Coming Home to Your True Self.* Downers Grove, Ill.: InterVarsity Press, 2008.

Lindsay, D. Michael. *Faith in the Halls of Power.* New York: Oxford University Press, 2007.

Lowney, Chris. *Heroic Leadership.* Chicago: Loyola Press, 2003.

Moreland, J. P. *Love God with All Your Mind.* Colorado Springs: NavPress, 1997.

Morse, MaryKate. *Making Room for Leadership.* Downers Grove, Ill.: InterVarsity Press, 2008.

Mulholland, M. Robert, Jr. *Invitation to a Journey.* Downers Grove: InterVarsity Press, 1993.

Nouwen, Henri J. M. *In the Name of Jesus.* New York: Crossroad, 1999.

Ogden, Greg, and Daniel Meyer. *Leadership Essentials.* Downers Grove, Ill.: InterVarsity Press, 2007.

Palmer, Parker. *Let Your Life Speak.* San Francisco: Jossey-Bass. 2000.

Peterson, Eugene H. *The Jesus Way.* Grand Rapids: Eerdmans, 2007.

———. *A Long Obedience in the Same Direction.* Downers Grove, Ill.: InterVarsity Press, 2000.

Smith, Gordon T. *The Voice of Jesus.* Downers Grove, Ill.: InterVarsity Press, 2003.

Thrall, Bill, Bruce McNicol and Ken McElrath. *The Ascent of a Leader.* San Francisco: Jossey-Bass, 1999.

Tokunaga, Paul. *Invitation to Lead.* Downers Grove, Ill.: InterVarsity Press, 2003.

White, John. *Excellence in Leadership.* Downers Grove, Ill.: InterVarsity Press, 1986.

Willard, Dallas. *Renovation of the Heart.* Colorado Springs: NavPress, 2002.

Wright, N. T. *The Challenge of Jesus.* Downers Grove, Ill.: InterVarsity Press, 1999.

ACKNOWLEDGMENTS

Neither leadership nor the spiritual life can be learned in a vacuum; both are necessarily dependent on numerous others. I have been so blessed by people throughout my life who have encouraged me in both my leadership and spiritual growth. I cannot list them all individually by name for fear of missing many. But I do want to acknowledge and thank the following groups of people for all that they have given to me.

First, I am thankful for those in the churches I have been part of for being faithful communities of God's people who taught and practiced fidelity to God and his Word. I think of my boyhood Sunday school teachers, who helped me to learn the Bible and encouraged me to preach and teach the Scriptures to others. I think of pastors and friends of seven different churches in five different states, who have welcomed and supported Alice and me in our ministry callings. Thank you all for your faithful support.

Second, I am indebted to all of my colleagues in InterVarsity Christian Fellowship. I have had the privilege of directly serving six presidents, and each of them has contributed greatly and uniquely to my spiritual and leadership development. I think of the hundreds of campus staff, staff directors, faculty, trustees and my current cabinet colleagues as all giving so much to me. Thank you all for all the fellowship, prayers and joint labors.

I particularly want to thank all those at InterVarsity Press who for more than twelve years have been a constant source of enjoyable partnership in this wonderful challenge of being a leading publisher of thoughtful Christian books. Thanks to the executive leadership team for your own leadership competence and help to me. I especially want to thank senior editor Cindy Bunch for your expertise and effective encouragement to me to write this book. Everyone at IVP is really part of this book, and I greatly appreciate you all.

I also want to express my gratitude and love to my family. Thanks to my brother John in leading me to the Lord and into InterVarsity, and for that gift of commentaries you gave to me when I graduated from college. You have always been an example of Christian leadership to me.

Thanks to my daughters, Dorie and Elisa, for all that you mean to me. You have led the way for me in already writing your own books, but you have also led me to be a better dad. I love you, your husbands and our grandchildren!

Finally, I want to thank my wife, Alice, for being my greatest human source of love, encouragement and inspiration. Your continual longing for God and uncompromising honesty have prompted and provided for my own spiritual growth in ways too numerous to list. Thank you for your faithfulness to me and to the Lord.

Indeed it is to the Lord from whom all blessings flow. To God be the glory.

NOTES

Introduction

p. 15   Carmen Bernos de Gasztold, "The Peacock," in *The Creatures'*
Choir, trans. Rumer Godden (New York: Penguin, 1976), pp.
108-9. Used by permission.

Chapter 1: A Weaned Soul

p. 31   Leo Braudy, *The Frenzy of Renown* (New York: Oxford University Press, 1986).

p. 33   "I want to love God": Henri J. M. Nouwen, *The Genesee Diary*
(London: Darton, Longman & Todd, 1981), p. 76.

p. 35   "He that commends me": William Shakespeare, "The Comedy
of Errors," in *The Complete Works of William Shakespeare* (Middlesex, U.K.: Hamlyn, 1958), p. 317.

p. 36   "No ancient society before the Jews": Thomas Cahill, *The Gifts*
of the Jews (New York: Doubleday, 1998), p. 144.

p. 39   "This isn't practicing": Philip Yancey, "What Art Can—and
Can't—Do," *First Things*, February 2009, p. 38.

p. 40   "The word busy is the symptom": Eugene Peterson, "The Unbusy Pastor," *Leadership*, summer 1981, p. 70.

p. 40   "You must ruthlessly eliminate hurry": John Ortberg, *The Life*
You've Always Wanted (Grand Rapids: Zondervan, 2002), p. 76.

Chapter 2: A Growing Strength

p. 45   "I recently read a biography of Andrew Jackson": Jon Meacham,
American Lion: Andrew Jackson in the White House (New York:
Random House, 2008).

p. 46   "just to take a pain": Doris Kearns Goodwin, *Team of Rivals*
(New York: Simon & Schuster, 2005), p. 104.

p. 47   "no one can be authentic": Bill George, *True North* (San Francisco: Jossey-Bass, 2007), p. xxvi.

p. 53   "the mother of all heretics": Augustine of Hippo, *Against the Fundamental Epistle of Manichaeus*, chap. 6.

p. 55   "The Accusative Case": Carolyn Nystrom. *John Calvin: Sovereign Hope* (Downers Grove, Ill.: InterVarsity Press, 2002), p. 7.

p. 58   "It is in giving": Francis of Assisi, *The Prayer of St. Francis*.

Chapter 3: A Renewed Mind

p. 62   "another battle in the cultural": N. T. Wright, address at the Following Christ conference, Chicago, December 31, 2008.

p. 62   "I am a Myers-Briggs 'T,'": The Myers-Briggs Type Indicator is a self-report questionnaire designed to make Jung's theory of psychological types understandable and useful in everyday life. Isabel Briggs Myers, *Introduction to Type* (Mountain View, Calif.: Consulting Psychologists Press Inc., 1998), p. 5.

p. 63   Henri J. M. Nouwen, "Descend with the Mind into the Heart," *Sojourners*, August 1980.

p. 64   "saw society as a shipwreck": Thomas Merton, *Wisdom of the Desert* (Boston: Shambhala, 1960), p. 1.

p. 68   "tells the story": N. T. Wright, "Correspondence," *First Things* 184 (2008).

p. 71   "there is not much of an": Mark A. Noll, *The Scandal of the Evangelical Mind* (Grand Rapids: Eerdmans, 1994), p. 3.

p. 71   "The contemporary Christian mind": J. P. Moreland, *Love God with All Your Mind* (Colorado Springs: NavPress, 1997), p. 80.

p. 71   "We need spiritual values": Pope John Paul II, "Religion," *Time*, December 11, 1989, p. 37.

pp. 71-72   "Make us ever mindful": Patrick Henry, *The Ironic Christian's Companion* (New York: Riverhead, 1999), p. 153.

p. 72   "in the total expanse of human": Abraham Kuyper, "Sphere Sovereignty," in *Abraham Kuyper: A Centennial Reader*, ed. James D. Bratt (Grand Rapids: Eerdmans, 1998), p. 488.

pp. 72-73   "God All Nature Sings Thy Glory": David Clowney, *Hymns II* (Downers Grove, Ill.: InterVarsity Press, 1976), p. 14.

pp. 74-75   "An example of a leader": Timothy Johnson and Peter Jennings in dinner reception, New York City, May 26, 2004.

pp. 77-78   "Largely through the example": John Stanford in personal communication, May 2009.

Chapter 4: A Dancing Heart

p. 79   "My heart was strangely warmed": John Wesley, *Journal of John Wesley* (Chicago: Moody Press, 1951), chap. 2.

p. 82   "While my mind obliged me to serve": Chris Armstrong, "When Details Get You Down," *Leadership*, winter 2009, p. 84.

p. 82   "He was able to formulate": Ibid.

p. 84   "Functional atheism": Parker Palmer, *Let Your Life Speak* (San Francisco: Jossey-Bass, 2000), p. 88.

p. 85   "True religion which 'consists'": Jonathan Edwards, *Religious Affections* (Portland, Ore.: Multnomah, 1984), p. 5.

p. 85   "Change their desires": Bill Cosby, interview on NPR's *Talk of the Nation*, May 3, 2005.

p. 86   "In a parade, really unequal beings": Robert Farrar Capon, *Bed and Board* (New York: Simon & Schuster, 1965), p. 54.

p. 86   "If I don't practice for one day": Ignacy Paderewski, Quotations Book website <http://quotationsbook.com/quote/31799/>.

pp. 88-89   "Good morning, Heavenly Father": John R. W. Stott, "Pottering and Prayer," *Christianity Today*, April 2, 2001, p. 61.

Chapter 5: In a Frenzied World

p. 99   "You're on our": *The New Yorker*, August 20, 2007, p. 58.

p. 100   "Sleep is a crutch": Anna Kuchment, "Make That a Double," *Newsweek*, July 30, 2007, p. 48.

p. 100   "sad fate of the comma": Robert Samuelson, "The Sad Fate of the Comma," *Newsweek*, July 23, 2007, p. 41.

pp. 103-4   "If an expert does not have": Chuang Tzu, as cited in Parker Palmer, "Active Life," *The Active Life* (New York: Harper & Row, 1990), p. 37.

Chapter 6: In a Lonely World

p. 118   "the republic of overwork": Quoted from the *Financial Times* by Robert J. Samuelson in "The Sad Fate of the Comma," *Newsweek*, July 23, 2007, p. 41.

p. 119   "the light is so much better here": Idries Shah, *The Pleasantries of the Incredible Mulla Nasrudin* (London: Octagon, 1983), p. 93, quoted in David Benner, *The Gift of Being Yourself* (Downers Grove, Ill.: InterVarsity Press, 2004), p. 59.

p. 120   "bored and busy": Henri Nouwen, *Lifesigns* (New York. Doubleday, 1989), p. 41.

p. 121   "noonday demon": Gerald Sittser, *Water from a Deep Well*

(Downers Grove, Ill..: InterVarsity Press, 2007), p. 116.

p. 122   "jumbo shrimp and the smallest": Charles Handy, *The Age of Paradox* (Cambridge, Mass.: Harvard University Press, 1994).

p. 123   "for you made us for yourself": Augustine of Hippo, *The Confessions of St. Augustine* (Uhrichsville, Ohio: Barbour, 1984), p. 5.

p. 124   "When everything is moving at once": Blaise Pascal, *Pensées* (Indianapolis: Hackett, 2004), p. 174.

p. 125   "Praise the Lord or change the world": William Wilberforce, quoted in the film *Amazing Grace* (2006).

p. 125   "It is hoped and believed": John Newton, quoted by Eric Metaxas in *Amazing Grace* (New York: HarperCollins, 2007), p. 68.

pp. 125-26   Ken Elzinga, in personal correspondence, May 18, 2009.

p. 130   "If you are a Christian": Flannery O'Connor, quoted in Jill P. Baumgaertner, "The Meaning Is in You," *Christian Century,* December 23-30, 1987, p. 1172.

p. 131   "To be a witness": Madeline L'Engle, *Walking on Water* (Wheaton, Ill.: Harold Shaw, 1980), p. 31.

Chapter 7: In a Fragmented World

p. 134   "99.9% identical": Francis Collins, *The Language of God* (New York: Free Press, 2006), pp. 125, 133-34.

p. 134   "A sense of Divinity": John Calvin, *Institutes of the Christian Religion* 59 (Philadelphia: Westminster Press, 1960), p. 26.

p. 135   "Thou didst make him": H. C. Leupold, *Exposition of the Psalms* (Minneapolis: Augsburg Press, 1961), p. 104.

p. 136   "Culture is said to be": Terry Eagleton, quoted in James Smith, *Terry Eagleton: A Critical Introduction* (Boston: Polity, 2008), p. 111.

p. 136   "An integrated system": Lausanne Committee on World Evangelization, Willowbank Report, 1974.

pp. 139-40   "condescendingly down on": Stephen Carter, *New England White* (New York: Vintage, 2008), p. 74.

p. 141   "mean and non-mean": Martin Marty, quoted in Krista Tippett, *Speaking of Faith* (New York: Viking, 2007), p. 161.

p. 142   "Shalom sometimes refers": Perry Yoder, *Shalom: The Bible's Word for Salvation, Justice, Peace* (Nappanee, Ind.: Evangel Publishing House, 1998), p. 16.

Chapter 8: As More Than a Grasshopper

p. 166   "In the coming world": Parker Palmer, *Let Your Life Speak* (San Francisco: Jossey-Bass, 2000), p. 11.

Chapter 9: As an Organizational Ecologist

p. 169   "a word derived from": Timothy George, in inauguration chapel service, Gordon-Conwell Theological Seminary, October 6, 2006.

pp. 170-71   "promoting excessive internal": Jean Lipman-Blumen, *The Allure of Toxic Leadership* (New York: Oxford University Press, 2005), p. 17.

p. 172   "Focused attention": Ross Campbell, *How to Really Love Your Child* (Colorado Springs: Cook Communications, 2003), p. 57.

p. 172   "the sacrament of the present moment": Jean-Pierre de Caussade, *The Sacrament of the Present Moment* (New York: HarperCollins, 1982), p. viii.

p. 173   "Paying attention is not": Leighton Ford, *The Attentive Life* (Downers Grove, Ill.: InterVarsity Press, 2008), p. 15.

p. 179   "to slow down": Jean Vanier, *Living Gently in a Violent World* (Downers Grove, Ill.: InterVarsity Press, 2008), p. 45.

Chapter 10: As a Grateful Creature

p. 188   "defining reality and": Max De Pree, *Leadership Is an Art* (East Lansing: Michigan State University Press, 1987), p. 11.

p. 191   "the specific pleasure": C. S. Lewis, *The Weight of Glory* (Grand Rapids: Eerdmans, 1965), pp. 9, 13.

p. 192   "leaders don't inflict pain": De Pree, *Leadership Is an Art*, p. 11.

p. 197   "as a place": Alice Fryling, *Seeking God Together* (Downers Grove, Ill.: InterVarsity Press, 2000), p. 8.

p. 197   "cultivating rhythms": Ruth Haley Barton, *Sacred Rhythms* (Downers Grove, Ill.: InterVarsity Press, 2006), p. 146.

p. 197   Anne Elizabeth McLoughlin, "Living a Little Rule of Life," *Conversations* 5, no. 2 (2007).

formatio
TRADITION. EXPERIENCE.
TRANSFORMATION.

Formatio books from InterVarsity Press follow the rich tradition of the church in the journey of spiritual formation. These books are not merely about being informed, but about being transformed by Christ and conformed to his image. Formatio stands in InterVarsity Press's evangelical publishing tradition by integrating God's Word with spiritual practice and by prompting readers to move from inward change to outward witness. InterVarsity Press uses the chambered nautilus for Formatio, a symbol of spiritual formation because of its continual spiral journey outward as it moves from its center. We believe that each of us is made with a deep desire to be in God's presence. Formatio books help us to fulfill our deepest desires and to become our true selves in light of God's grace.